In Touch

A BEGINNING AMERICAN ENGLISH SERIES

Student's Book 2

OSCAR CASTRO • VICTORIA KIMBROUGH

Project Coordinator: Lyn McLean • Developmental Editor: Larry Anger
Consultants: Russell N. Campbell and William E. Rutherford

Longman

imnrc

IN TOUCH, Student's Book 2

First printing 1980
5   4   3   2

ISBN 0 582 79746 2
Library of Congress Catalog Card Number: 79-24918

Project Editor: Marcie Miller
Character Illustrations: M.J. Quay
Cover Design: Frederick Charles Ltd.
Cover Photography: Gayle Covner, Ross O'Loughlin, Oscar Castro, Victoria Kimbrough
Design: Robert Fitzpatrick/Flex, Inc.

We wish to thank the following for providing us with photographs:
Page 2: Angel L. Cuevas. **Page 4:** Gayle Covner. **Page 20:** the Cosmos. **Page 21,** left: the Cosmos; right: the New York Knickerbockers. **Page 25,** top: the Port Authority of New York and New Jersey; bottom: New York Convention and Visitors Bureau. **Page 26:** the Port Authority of New York and New Jersey. **Page 28,** top: Rockefeller Center, Inc.; bottom left: United Nations; bottom right: New York Convention and Visitors Bureau. **Page 48:** the Port Authority of New York and New Jersey. **Page 49:** Angel L. Cuevas. **Page 74:** Angel L. Cuevas. **Page 77:** Angel L. Cuevas. **Page 82:** DC Comics Inc. **Page 84:** Angel L. Cuevas. **Page 107:** Angel L. Cuevas. **Page 113:** the New York Public Library Picture Collection/Metro-Goldwyn-Mayer Inc.

We also wish to thank the following artists:
Page 14: Anna Veltfort. **Page 19:** Ted Enik. **Page 37:** Ted Enik. **Page 41:** Leland Neff. **Page 50:** Ted Enik. **Page 51:** T/A Creations. **Page 52:** Leland Neff. **Page 58:** Leland Neff. **Page 62:** Anna Veltfort. **Page 66:** Anna Veltfort. **Page 86:** Ted Enik. **Page 90:** Anna Veltfort.

Printed in the U.S.A.

Longman Inc.
19 West 44th Street
New York, New York 10036
U.S.A.

Instituto Mexicano Norteamericano
de Relaciones Culturales, A.C.
Hamburgo 115
México 6, D.F.

Acknowledgements

We wish to acknowledge the valuable cooperation of the teaching and administrative staff of the Instituto Mexicano Norteamericano de Relaciones Culturales in Mexico City during the writing of this course.

We also wish to acknowledge the teachers who field-tested these materials: Luis Abreu, Isabelle Marchese and Treasa Phillips.

We were very fortunate to have the help of Rafael Barajas Durán, who illustrated the pilot edition, Ninfa Gonzalez, Mary Martin and Alicia Valenzuela, who helped prepare the manuscript, and Cris Grana and Dorothy Niemczyk for their assistance during production.

Jean Bodman and Milton G. Saltzer of the American Language Institute at New York University were extremely helpful in granting permission to use the Institute as a setting for the book.

We would especially like to thank Jane Sturtevant, Frank Lozano and Marcie Miller for their invaluable suggestions and contributions; Brian Abbs and Ingrid Freebairn for permitting us to adapt their Language Summary in *Starting Strategies* (Longman Group Ltd., London, 1978) and Adrian Palmer and Margot Kimball for allowing us to adapt their Dialog Game in *Getting Along in English* (Longman Inc., New York, 1981).

We are also very grateful to all our friends and colleagues who encouraged and supported us.

Oscar Castro
Victoria Kimbrough

New York and Mexico 1980

Introducing...

Ernesto Costa, Tony's uncle, has been in New York for ten years. He owns a Brazilian restaurant on 45th Street.

Paula Duran is a newspaper reporter for the New York News. She just moved to New York from Chicago. She and Tony are neighbors.

Tomiko Sato and Tony Costa go out together. They met at the American Language Institute at New York University where they study English. Tony's from Brazil. He works part time in his uncle's restaurant. Tomiko's from Japan and works part time as a secretary for Japan Air Lines. She lives with her cousin Toshi and his American wife Lynn.

Maria Sanchez came to New York from Mexico to study English and hotel administration. She's in the same class as Tony and Tomiko.

Ali Helal is one of Tony's friends. He's from Egypt and came to New York to study English.

Jim Chapman teaches English at the American Language Institute. Sue Cleveland is a secretary there. Tomiko, Tony, Maria and Ali are all in Jim Chapman's class.

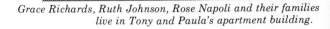

Grace Richards, Ruth Johnson, Rose Napoli and their families live in Tony and Paula's apartment building.

Contents

UNIT 1
I'd like you to meet Grace Richards.

It's Friday morning. Tony's on his way to play tennis when he meets two women who live in his apartment building.

GRACE:	Who's that? Do you know him?
RUTH:	Uh-huh. That's Tony Costa. He's from Brazil.
GRACE:	Oh, really? What does he do?
RUTH:	He studies English at New York University and I think he works for his uncle. Come on. I'll introduce you. . . . Good morning, Tony.
TONY:	Oh, hi, Mrs. Johnson. How are you?
RUTH:	Fine. Tony, I'd like you to meet Grace Richards.
TONY:	It's nice to meet you, Mrs. Richards.
GRACE:	Nice to meet you too. Ruth tells me you're from Brazil.
TONY:	Uh-huh.
GRACE:	How long have you been here?
TONY:	For about three months.
RUTH:	Is that all? Your English is so good!

TONY:	Thanks. I studied in Brazil for a couple of years.
GRACE:	Oh.
TONY:	Say, do you know what time it is?
RUTH:	It's quarter after nine.
TONY:	Excuse me?
RUTH:	9:15.
TONY:	Oh, I've got to go. I've got to meet Tomiko at 9:30. It was nice to meet you, Mrs. Richards.
GRACE:	Nice to meet you too.
RUTH:	See you later, Tony.

Answer *That's right* **or** *That's wrong.*

1. Grace knows Tony.
2. Tony's a teacher at New York University.
3. *Uh-huh* means "yes."
4. Tony has lived in New York for three months.

1

PRACTICE 1   Ask and say who people are. Ask about their occupations.

GRACE: Who's that? Do you know him?
RUTH: Uh-huh. That's Tony Costa.
GRACE: What does he do?
RUTH: He studies English at New York University and I think he works for his uncle.

A: Who's that? Do you know him/her/them?
B: Uh-huh. That's .... *or* No, I don't.

If someone answers *yes,* **you can continue like this:**

A: What does/do ....do?
B: ....

> *You can say:*
>
> He's a student./They're students.
> She studies at New York University./
>   They study at New York University.

PRACTICE 2   Introduce other people like this:

RUTH: Tony, I'd like you to meet Grace Richards.
TONY: It's nice to meet you, Mrs. Richards.
GRACE: Nice to meet you too.

A: ...., I'd like you to meet ....
B: It's nice to meet you, ...
C: Nice to meet you too.

PRACTICE 3   Ask someone how long he/she has been here.
Say how long you've been here.

GRACE: How long have you been here?
TONY: For about three months.

A: How long have you .... here?
B: (For) ....

> *You can also ask and answer:*
>
> | How long have you **lived** here? | Since August. |
> | **worked** | Since 1978. |
> | **studied** | Since last week. |

PRACTICE 4   Ask what time it is. Tell someone the time.

TONY: Do you know what time it is?
RUTH: It's 9:15.

A: Do you know what time it is?
B: (It's) ....

NOTE:

9:00   It's nine o'clock.   9:15   It's nine fifteen or quarter after nine.   9:30   It's nine thirty.   9:45   It's nine forty-five or quarter to ten.

PRACTICE 5 — Say you have to leave and say goodbye to someone you've just met like this:

TONY: I've got to go. I've got to meet Tomiko at 9:30.
It was nice to meet you, Mrs. Richards.
GRACE: Nice to meet you too, Tony.

A: I've got to go. I've got to ....
It was nice to meet you, ...
B: Nice to meet you too, ...

PRACTICE 6 — Write *do/don't* **or** *does/doesn't*.

GRACE: Who's Tomiko?
RUTH: Excuse me?
GRACE: Who's Tomiko?
RUTH: Oh, she's Tony's girlfriend.
GRACE: She has an unusual name. Where's she from?
RUTH: Japan, I think.
GRACE: .... she study at NYU too?
RUTH: I .... know. I .... see Tony very often and he .... talk about her very much.
GRACE: Tony seems nice.
RUTH: Yeah, I know.
GRACE: .... he have any other relatives in New York?
RUTH: No, just his aunt and uncle.
GRACE: What .... they do?
RUTH: They have a restaurant.
GRACE: Say, ... you have time for a cup of coffee?
RUTH: Not right now. Maybe later.
GRACE: OK. See you.

NOTE:

If you don't understand something or if you didn't hear, you can say:
Excuse me?

PRACTICE 7 — Open Conversation

A: .... , I'd like you to meet ....

B: ....

C: Nice to meet you too.

B: Where are .... ?

C: ....

B: How long .... ?

C: ....

EXPANSION

Dear Pamela

(1) **Dear Pamela:** I've been dating a very attractive, well-educated foreign student. I know he comes from a good family because in general his manners
(5) are perfect. However, there is one thing that bothers me. Thomas (not his real name) touches everyone he talks to. He puts his arm around other men and every time he talks to a woman he
(10) takes her arm or just stands too close. It makes everybody nervous. My friends and family are uncomfortable with him and I'm embarrassed. Why does he do this? Doesn't he understand
(15) it's rude? Should I tell him or should I stop seeing him?

—"Embarrassed"

Dear Embarrassed: In many countries (20) touching is more common than it is in the United States. People always shake hands when they see each other. Sometimes they put their arms around each other when they walk down the street, and they often kiss when they say hello or goodbye. Often people from these
(25) countries think Americans are cold and unfriendly because they don't touch each other very much. Your boyfriend probably feels that touching is a way to show friendship. If this bothers you,
(30) you should explain to him that here two men will probably shake hands when they meet, but otherwise they don't usually touch each other. Men don't touch women very much either unless
(35) they're dating or married. When you talk to him, be diplomatic. Let him know you're trying to help, not criticize.

PRACTICE 8   Read the letters and circle the answers.

1. In lines (5) and (6) *there is one thing that bothers me* means

   a) there is one thing the writer likes about Thomas.
   b) there is one thing the writer doesn't like about Thomas.

2. In line (11) *it* refers to

   a) touching.
   b) the foreign student.

3. In lines (11) and (12) *My friends and family are uncomfortable* probably means

   a) my friends and family feel good.
   b) my friends and family feel bad.

4. In line (13) *I'm embarrassed* probably means

   a) I feel good.
   b) I feel bad.

5. In line (14) *this* refers to

   a) touching people.
   b) talking to friends and family.

6. In line (15) *rude* probably means

   a) something that's good.
   b) something that's bad.

7. *"Embarrassed"* is

   a) a man.
   b) a woman.

8. In lines (20) and (21) *People always shake hands when they see each other* refers to

   a) people in the United States.
   b) people in other countries.

9. In line (30) *this* refers to

   a) the boyfriend.
   b) touching.

4

PRACTICE 9 There are four sentences in the following paragraph. Capitalize and punctuate them.

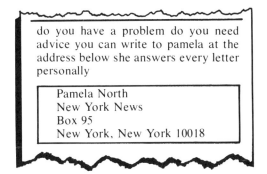

do you have a problem do you need advice you can write to pamela at the address below she answers every letter personally

Pamela North
New York News
Box 95
New York, New York 10018

PRACTICE 10 Tony's on his way to meet Tomiko.
Listen and answer *That's right* or *That's wrong.*

1. Tony and Nancy are friends.

2. Ali and Nancy are friends.

3. Ali and Tony are friends.

HOW MUCH DO YOU KNOW?

1. Complete the Conversation

GRACE: ....?

RUTH: That's Tony Costa.

GRACE: ....?

RUTH: He studies English at New York University. Come on. I'll introduce you. Hi, Tony.

TONY: ....

RUTH: Tony, ...

TONY: Nice to meet you, Mrs. Richards.

GRACE: ....

RUTH: Tony's from Brazil.

GRACE: Oh, really? ....
.... in New York?

TONY: About three months.

2. Find the Conversation

There is one conversation here. Read it with your partner. You read part **A** and cover part **B**. Your partner reads part **B** and covers part **A**. Listen to your partner before you answer.

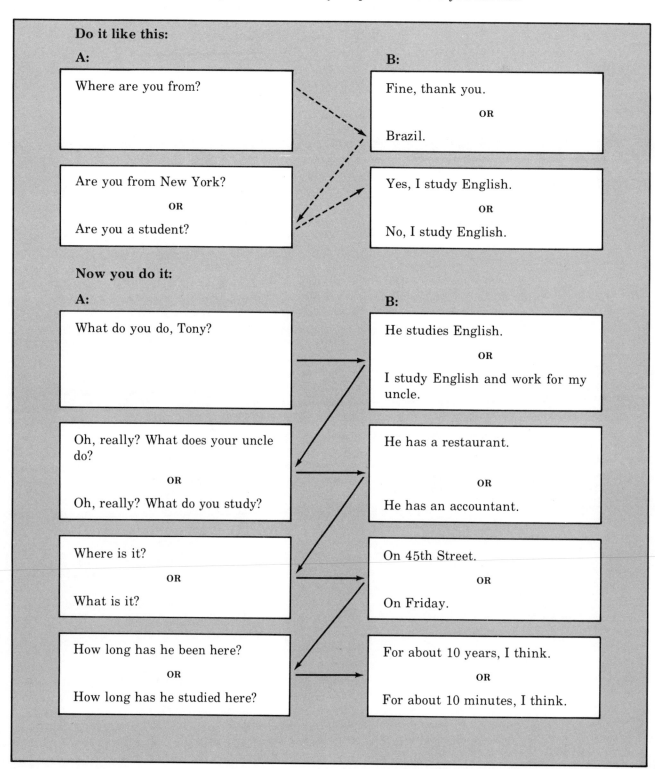

Do it like this:

A:

Where are you from?

Are you from New York?

OR

Are you a student?

B:

Fine, thank you.

OR

Brazil.

Yes, I study English.

OR

No, I study English.

Now you do it:

A:

What do you do, Tony?

Oh, really? What does your uncle do?

OR

Oh, really? What do you study?

Where is it?

OR

What is it?

How long has he been here?

OR

How long has he studied here?

B:

He studies English.

OR

I study English and work for my uncle.

He has a restaurant.

OR

He has an accountant.

On 45th Street.

OR

On Friday.

For about 10 years, I think.

OR

For about 10 minutes, I think.

3. Circle the Answer

1. A: How are you?
   B: ....
      a) And you? b) OK, I guess. c) Nice to meet you.

2. A: Who's that?
   B: ....
      a) That's my book. b) That's Tomiko. c) That's right.

3. A: What does he do?
   B: ....
      a) He's from Brazil. b) He's all right. c) He's a student.

4. A: How long have you lived here?
   B: ....
      a) For two years. b) At four o'clock. c) In New York.

5. A: I've got to go now.
   B: ....
      a) Hi. b) That's a good idea. c) Bye.

6. A: I'd like you to meet Tony Costa.
   B: ....
      a) Nice to meet you too. b) Nice to meet you. c) Thank you.

LANGUAGE SUMMARY

Now You Can Do This:

introduce people:	Tony, I'd like you to meet Grace Richards. It's nice to meet you, Mrs. Richards.
ask and say how long:	How long have you been here? For about three months.
identify other people:	Who's that? Do you know him? Uh-huh. That's Tony Costa.
ask and say what other people do:	What does he do? He studies English at New York University.
ask and tell someone the time:	Do you know what time it is? It's 9:15.
say you have to leave and say why:	I've got to go. I've got to meet Tomiko at 9:30.
say goodbye to people you've just met:	It was nice to meet you, Mrs. Richards. Nice to meet you too, Tony.

Grammar

Present Perfect

How long **have** you	been worked lived studied	here?	For about three months.

Present Tense

I You We They	**study**	English.
He She	**studies**	

Present Tense: Questions

What **do** you What **does** he/she	**study?**	English.

Have got to/Has got to

I You We They	**'ve got to**	go.
He She	**'s got to**	meet Tomiko.

Object Pronouns

Do you know	**him?** **her?** **them?**	Yes. That's Tony Costa. Yes. That's Grace Richards. Yes. That's Mr. and Mrs. Richards.

Useful Words and Expressions

studies/have studied (study)*	•	•	Mrs.	since
was/have been (be)	years	him	•	•
has (have)	week	them	how long	Uh-huh.
have got to	uncle	•	•	

    * base form of the verb

UNIT 2 · What's the matter?

Tony's waiting for Tomiko and she's late.

TOMIKO: I'm sorry I'm late, but I don't feel very well.

TONY: You don't look very good either. What's the matter?

TOMIKO: I guess I have a cold. I feel terrible. I have a headache and a sore throat.

TONY: Gee, that's too bad. Why don't you go home and go to bed? Or maybe you should see a doctor.

TOMIKO: No, I'll be OK. But I don't feel like going to class tonight, so could you give this note to Mr. Chapman?

TONY: Sure, I'd be glad to. I hope you feel better.

TOMIKO: Thanks.

Answer *That's right* **or** *That's wrong.*

1. Tony's late.
2. Tony is sorry that Tomiko has a cold.
3. Tony wants Tomiko to give a note to Mr. Chapman.

PRACTICE 1   Say you don't feel well and say what's wrong.

TOMIKO: I don't feel very well.
TONY: What's the matter?
TOMIKO: I guess I have a cold.

A: I don't feel very well/good.
B: What's the matter?
A: I have a/an ....

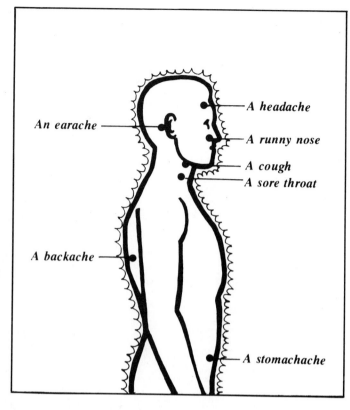

A headache
An earache
A runny nose
A cough
A sore throat
A backache
A stomachache

PRACTICE 2   Say you don't feel well. Suggest what to do if someone doesn't feel well.

TOMIKO: I have a headache and a sore throat.
TONY: Gee, that's too bad. Why don't you go home and go to bed?
TOMIKO: That's a good idea.

A: I have a ....
B: (Gee), that's too bad. Why don't you ....?
    or Maybe you should ....
A: That's a good idea. *or* No, I'll be OK.

You can say:	
Why don't you	go home?
	go to bed?
	see a doctor?
Maybe you should	take some aspirin.
	lie down.
	get some rest.

PRACTICE 3   Say you don't want to do something and say why.

TOMIKO: I don't feel like going to class tonight.
TONY: Why not?
TOMIKO: Because I don't feel well.

A: I don't feel like _____-ing ....
B: Why not?
A: (Because) I ....

If someone is sick, you can continue like this:

B: I hope you feel better.
A: Thanks.

You can also say:	
(Because)	I'm sick.
	I'm tired.
	I cut myself.
	I burned myself.
	I hurt my back.
	I have a cold.

PRACTICE 4 Ask someone to do something for you.
Say you can or can't do something for someone.

TOMIKO: Could you give this note to Mr. Chapman?
TONY: Sure. I'd be glad to.

A: Could you give .... to ....?
B: Sure. I'd be glad to. *or* I'm sorry, I can't.

NOTE:
I'd be glad to.
I'd = I would.

PRACTICE 5   Write *should, could, do/don't* **or** *does/doesn't.*

ALI: Where's Tomiko?
TONY: She .... feel well. She has a cold.
ALI: That's too bad. She .... go to the doctor.
TONY: I know. .... you know a good one?
ALI: Uh-huh.
TONY: .... you give me the phone number?
ALI: I .... have it with me.
TONY: Well, why .... you call Tomiko later and give it to her?
ALI: Sure. I'd be glad to.

PRACTICE 6   Open Conversation

A: What's the matter?
B: I don't feel well. I have a ....
A: Maybe you should ....
B: That's a good idea.
A: I hope ....
B: ....

EXPANSION

The Common Cold

It's October again and one out of every ten people in the United States is sick with a cold. Just what is a cold? In general, when you have a cold you feel very tired. You probably have a runny nose and a sore throat and maybe you have a headache, a stomachache or a fever.

What can you do?

Everyone has some kind of remedy—from orange juice to vitamin C. Some people take lemon juice and honey or drink hot tea. Others recommend a lot of rest and liquids. Aspirin is also a popular remedy. According to Dr. Jacobson, a famous cold specialist, you shouldn't work. You should go to bed and rest and take aspirin and vitamin C.

PRACTICE 7 Read the newspaper article and write the answers.

1.

> Everyone has some kind of remedy—from orange juice to vitamin C. Some people take lemon juice and honey or drink hot tea. Others recommend a lot of rest and liquids. Aspirin is also a popular remedy. According to Dr. Jacobson, a famous cold specialist.

A remedy is:

a) something to drink.

b) something to help you when you are sick.

Suggest some remedies for a stomachache.

a) ....

b) ....

2.

> honey or drink hot tea. Others recommend a lot of rest and liquids. Aspirin is

Orange juice is a liquid. Find other examples of liquids in the article.

a) ....

b) ....

PRACTICE 8 Talk about cold remedies like this:

A: When I have a cold, I ....

B: I .... (too).

NOTE:		
I take	aspirin. vitamins. medicine.	
I drink	orange juice. tea.	

PRACTICE 9 Read this note to Mr. Chapman. Then write a note to your teacher or boss. Explain why you can't go to school or work.

October 19, 1979

Dear Mr. Chapman,
I can't come to class tonight because I have an awful cold. Tony can tell me about class and give me the homework assignment.
I'll see you on Monday.

Tomiko Sato

_____, 19 ____

Dear _____,

_____

_____

_____

_____

_____

_____

_____

_____

_____

_____

PRACTICE 10 Listen to the telephone conversation and decide which symptoms describe Tomiko. Write her name in the blank.

JOHN BURNSIDE, M.D.
342 MADISON AVENUE
NEW YORK, NEW YORK 10017
682-9987

Date: 10/19/79   Time: 10:30 A.M.

_____ called.

Remarks: Has cold symptoms — headache, sore throat — but no fever. Prescribed 2 aspirin every 4 hours and rest. Will call tomorrow if not better.

JOHN BURNSIDE, M.D.
342 MADISON AVENUE
NEW YORK, NEW YORK 10017
682-9987

Date: 10/19/79   Time: 10:30 A.M.

_____ called.

Remarks: Has cold symptoms — sore throat, headache, diarrhea. Fever 101°. Prescribed aspirin every 4 hours.

PRACTICE 11 Do the crossword puzzle.

ACROSS

1. An article.
6. A cold symptom.
7. *You don't feel well* means you're
   ....
10. I have a cold. I feel ....
12. 12 DOWN.
13. What's the ....?
16. A pronoun.
17. Something to take for a cold.
20. A preposition.
21. The doctor told me .... take vitamin C for a cold.
22. A possessive adjective.
23. Nice to .... you.
24. A number between 5 and 15.

DOWN

1. *be: am, is,* ....
2. I don't .... well.
3. I hope you feel ....
4. Hello.
5. All right.
7. I'm .... I'm late.
8. Saturday and Sunday.
9. A cold symptom.

11. That's too .... I hope you feel better.
12. You and I.
14. A sore ....
15. I'm sorry I'm ....
16. 4 DOWN.
18. I have a .... throat.
19. Is not.
22. .... doesn't feel well.

HOW MUCH DO YOU KNOW?

1. Complete the Conversation

TOMIKO: I don't feel very good.

TONY: ....?

TOMIKO: I have an awful headache.

TONY: .... and go to bed?

TOMIKO: That's a good idea.

TONY: ....

TOMIKO: Thanks. Goodbye.

TONY: ....

"What's the matter?"

2. Find the Conversation

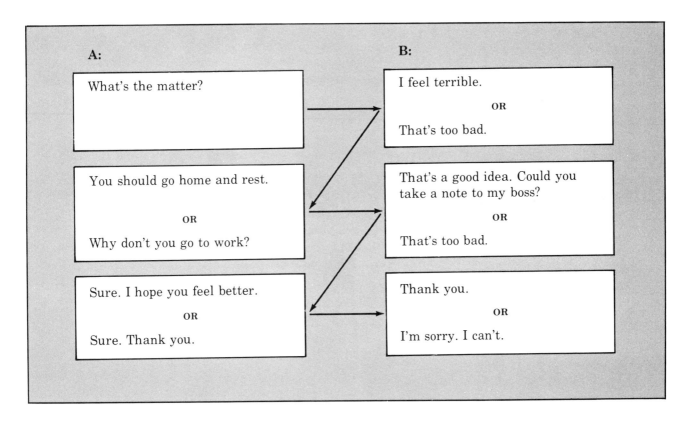

A:

What's the matter?

You should go home and rest.

OR

Why don't you go to work?

Sure. I hope you feel better.

OR

Sure. Thank you.

B:

I feel terrible.

OR

That's too bad.

That's a good idea. Could you take a note to my boss?

OR

That's too bad.

Thank you.

OR

I'm sorry. I can't.

3. Circle the Answer

1. A: I have an awful cold.
   B: ....
      a) That's nice.   b) Why don't you go home?   c) I feel good too.

2. A: I don't feel like going to work.
   B: ....
      a) When?   b) Why?   c) Where?

3. A: I hope you feel better.
   B: ....
      a) Why don't you take an aspirin?   b) That's a good idea.   c) Thank you.

4. A: What's the matter?
   B: ....
      a) I like her.   b) I'm from Mexico.   c) I have a cold.

5. A: Could you give this note to Mr. Chapman?
   B: ....
      a) No, I'll be OK.   b) I don't feel like going to a movie.   c) Sure. I'd be glad to.

LANGUAGE SUMMARY

Now You Can Do This:

talk about sickness:	I don't feel very well. What's the matter? I have a cold. I hope you feel better. Thanks.
say you don't feel like doing something:	I don't feel like going to class today.
make a suggestion:	Why don't you go home and go to bed? Maybe you should see a doctor.
accept a suggestion:	That's a good idea.
reject a suggestion:	No, I'll be OK.
make a request:	Could you give this note to Mr. Chapman?
agree to a request:	Sure. I'd be glad to.

Grammar

Well/Good and **Better**

I don't feel	**well/good.**
I hope you feel	**better.**

Feel like + -ing

I don't feel like going.
I don't feel like working.

Why/Because

I don't feel like going to class tonight.	**Why (not)?**	**Because** I'm sick.

Useful Words and Expressions

'll (will)	give	sore throat	•	•
should	cut (cut)	stomachache	well	when
•	hurt (hurt)	bed	bad	because
guess	•	aspirin	sick	•
rest	cold	home	tired	Gee.
burn	back	class	terrible	What's the matter?
hope	earache	note	•	I'd be glad to.
feel like	backache	boss	very	
see	headache	rest	sure	
take	runny nose	•	maybe	
lie down	cough	myself	tonight	

Did you have a nice weekend?

*Ali, Tomiko and Maria are talking
before class on Monday.*

ALI:	Where were you last Friday?
TOMIKO:	I was sick so I didn't come to class.
ALI:	That's too bad. What was the matter?
TOMIKO:	Oh, I had a cold. I stayed home all weekend. How was class?
MARIA:	It was kind of boring.
ALI:	Yeah, you didn't miss anything.
TOMIKO:	Did you have a nice weekend?
ALI:	Yes. I went to the Bears' game.
TOMIKO:	How about you, Maria?
MARIA:	A friend and I went to the movies. How was the game?
ALI:	I thought it was great. The Bears won.
MARIA:	What was the score?

ALI:	4 to 1.
TOMIKO:	What movie did you see?
MARIA:	*In Love Again.*
TOMIKO:	Was it good?
MARIA:	Yeah. We really enjoyed it.

Answer *That's right* **or** *That's wrong.*

1. Tomiko went to class on Friday.

2. Maria went to class on Friday.

3. Maria and a friend went to see the Bears.

4. *In Love Again* was good.

PRACTICE 1   Ask where someone was. Say where you were.

ALI: Where were you last Friday?
TOMIKO: I was sick.

A: Where were you ....?
B: ....

You can continue like this:

A: What was the matter?
B: I ....

NOTE:	
on	Sunday Monday Tuesday Wednesday
last	Thursday Friday Saturday
this morning/afternoon last week/night/month/year yesterday yesterday morning/afternoon	

PRACTICE 2   Ask for someone's opinion. Give your opinion.

TOMIKO: How was class on Friday?
MARIA: It was kind of boring.

A: How was ....?
B: It was kind of boring. *or* It was interesting/good.

PRACTICE 3   Ask about someone's weekend. Say what you did over the weekend.

TOMIKO: Did you have a nice weekend?
ALI: Yes. I went to the Bears' game. How about you?
TOMIKO: I stayed home all weekend.

A: Did you have a nice weekend?
B: Yes/No. I .... How about you?
A: ....

If someone saw a movie/TV program/play/game, you can continue like this:

B: What .... did you see?
A: ....

NOTE:	
Present	**Past**
play watch stay study visit	play**ed** soccer watch**ed** TV stay**ed** home stud**ied** for my test visit**ed** my aunt
go see take think	**went** to the movies **saw** *In Love Again* **took** a tour **thought** it was terrific

PRACTICE 4   Ask if someone liked what he/she did.

MARIA: How was the game?
ALI: I thought it was great.

A: How was ....? *or* Was .... good?
B: I/We thought it was great/terrible. *or* I/We really enjoyed it.

PRACTICE 5 — Write Maria's part of the conversation.

(Ask Tony how he is.)

MARIA: ....?
TONY: All right, thanks.

(Ask Tony if he had a nice weekend.)

MARIA: ....?
TONY: No, I stayed home and studied all weekend. How was your weekend?

(Tell him you and a friend went to the movies on Sunday. Tell him you saw *In Love Again*.)

MARIA: ....
....
TONY: Did you like it?

(Tell him you thought it was pretty interesting.)

MARIA: ....
....

PRACTICE 6 — Open Conversation

A: Where were you ....?
B: I .... How was class?
A: ....
B: Did you have a nice weekend?
A: Yes/No. I .... How about you?
B: I ....

"Did you have a nice weekend?"

E X P A N S I O N

Soccer News

Bears Win 2–1

(1)   The Bears beat the Greens last night in one of the most exciting games of the season. The score was tied one to one until the last 60 seconds of the game.
(5)   Then Bear forward Steve Ryan got the ball. Ryan kicked the ball right between the goalie's legs giving the Bears a final score of 2.
      Ryan, 22, has been with the Bears for
(10) one year. He's made 23 goals this season and has become the team's most valuable player. "I had a lot to learn when I began playing with the Bears," said the young forward from Florida,
(15) "and my teammates have really helped me."

Next week the Bears play the Pirates in New York City. If they win the game with the Pirates, the Bears will play in
(20) the championship tournament.

PRACTICE 7   Circle the answers.

1. "The Bears" is the name of

   a) a team.
   b) a sport.

2. In line (3) *The score was tied* means

   a) both teams had the same score.
   b) one team had more points than the other.

3. *Then Bear forward Steve Ryan got the ball* means

   a) Steve Ryan got the ball when there were about 55 seconds more in the game.
   b) Steve Ryan got the ball when there were 2 minutes more in the game.

4. In this article a *team* is

   a) a group of people who play soccer.
   b) a group of people who like soccer.

5. In lines (11) and (12) *most valuable* probably means

   a) best.
   b) worst.

6. The final score was

   a) Bears 1, Greens 2.
   b) Bears 2, Greens 1.

PRACTICE 8   Read the scores like this:

The Bears won   2 to 1

or

The Greens lost   1 to 2

Soccer Results

Bears	2
Greens	1
Warriors	4
Broncos	2

Basketball Results

Tigers	96
Hawks	95
Pumas	85
Trotters	72
Eagles	70
Lions	50
Pirates	75
Dolphins	68

PRACTICE 9   Put these sentences in the correct order to complete the paragraph.

The Eagles beat the Lions last night in the most exciting basketball game of the season.

.... After the game we interviewed Richards.

.... The game ended with the Eagles winning 70 to 50.

__1__ With only 5 seconds to play, Eagles' center Roger Richards got the ball.

.... Richards answered, "I just did what the coach told me."

.... He looked around and then threw it down the court and made a basket in the last second of the game.

.... We asked him how it felt to make the winning basket.

PRACTICE 10

Listen to the sports commentator and fill in the scoreboard. Then circle the team that won.

HOW MUCH DO YOU KNOW?

1. Complete the Conversation

TOMIKO: ....?

ALI: Yes, I went to the movies.

TOMIKO: ....?

ALI: *Doctors and Nurses.*

TOMIKO: ....?

ALI: I thought it was great. Did you have a nice weekend?

TOMIKO: ....

2. Find the Conversation

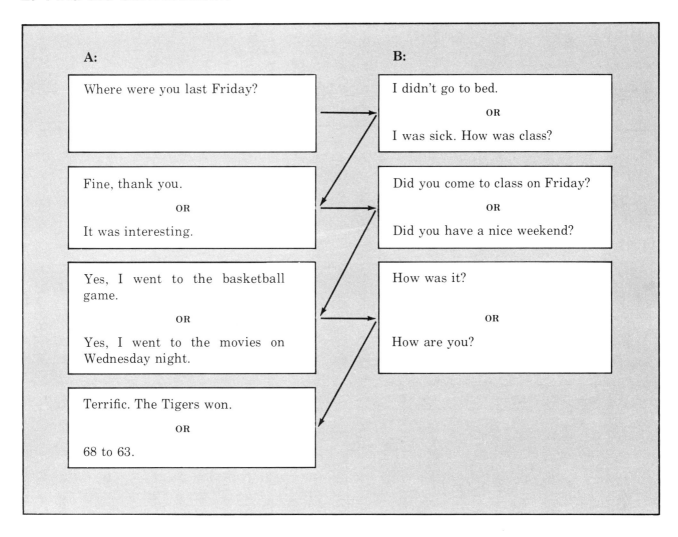

A:

> Where were you last Friday?

> Fine, thank you.
>
> **OR**
>
> It was interesting.

> Yes, I went to the basketball game.
>
> **OR**
>
> Yes, I went to the movies on Wednesday night.

> Terrific. The Tigers won.
>
> **OR**
>
> 68 to 63.

B:

> I didn't go to bed.
>
> **OR**
>
> I was sick. How was class?

> Did you come to class on Friday?
>
> **OR**
>
> Did you have a nice weekend?

> How was it?
>
> **OR**
>
> How are you?

3. Circle the Answer

1. A: Where were you last Friday?
   B: ....
   a) I was sick. b) I was wrong. c) I don't know.

2. A: How was class?
   B: ....
   a) Very well, thank you. b) All right, I guess. And you? c) It was OK.

3. A: Did you have a nice weekend?
   B: ....
   a) Yeah, I like sports. b) Yeah, I went to a football game. c) Yeah, I work and study.

4. A: What movie did you see?
   B: ....
   a) Last night. b) At the Logan Theater. c) *No Time for Love.*

5. A: How was the game?
   B: ....
   a) It was comfortable. b) Terrific. How about you? c) We really enjoyed it.

LANGUAGE SUMMARY

Now You Can Do This:

ask for and give information about the past:

Where were you last Friday? I was sick so I didn't come to class.
Did you have a nice weekend? Yes, I went to the Bears' game.

ask for and give an opinion:

How was class on Friday? It was kind of boring.
Was the movie good? It was great./We really enjoyed it.

Grammar

Past Tense of **Be: was/were**

Statements		
I/He/She	**was**	sick last Friday.
You/We/They	**were**	

Yes/No Questions	→ And Short Answers
Was the movie good?	Yes, it **was.** No, it **wasn't.**
Were they sick?	Yes, they **were.** No, they **weren't.**

Past Tense of Other Verbs

Regular Verbs

Base Form	Past	Base Form	Past
enjoy	enjoy**ed**	stay	stay**ed**
learn	learn**ed**	study	stud**ied**
like	lik**ed**	visit	visit**ed**
miss	miss**ed**	watch	watch**ed**
play	play**ed**		

Irregular Verbs *

Base Form	Past	Base Form	Past
come	**came**	see	**saw.**
do	**did**	take	**took**
go	**went**	think	**thought**
have	**had**	throw	**threw**
hear	**heard**	win	**won**
know	**knew**		

Statements		
I He/She We You They	enjoy**ed** **saw**	the movie.

Yes/No Questions		→ And Short Answers
Did you	enjoy see	the movie?

Yes, I **did.**
No, I **didn't.**

* For a complete list of irregular verbs, see page 119.

Time Expressions

on	Sunday	Thursday
	Monday	Friday
last	Tuesday	Saturday
	Wednesday	

this morning/afternoon

last night/week/month/year

yesterday/yesterday morning/yesterday afternoon

Useful Words and Expressions

			basketball	Wednesday	great
			game	Thursday	interesting
			weekend	Friday	terrific
enjoy	went (go)	thought (think)	Sunday	Saturday	boring
stay	were (be)	lost (lose)	Monday	•	•
did (do)	won (win)	•	Tuesday		kind of

Where did you go?

It's Monday evening. Jim Chapman is talking to Sue after class.

SUE: Hi, Jim. How are you?

JIM: Pretty good, and you?

SUE: Oh, fine. What did you do this weekend?

JIM: I went sightseeing with my kids.

SUE: Oh, where did you go?

JIM: We went to the zoo in Central Park and the United Nations. And then we went to the Statue of Liberty.

SUE: Did you go to the World Trade Center?

JIM: No. I thought about going, but my kids were tired, so we went to get something to eat instead. Have you been to the top?

SUE: Uh-huh. My husband and I went last year. The view's fabulous.

JIM: Well, maybe we can go next weekend.

SUE: Say, why don't we all go? I'd love to go back. And I'd like to meet your kids.

JIM: That's a good idea. Then let's go to Chinatown for dinner. On me!

SUE: Terrific!

Answer *That's right* **or** *That's wrong.*

1. Sue has been to the World Trade Center.

2. Sue knows Jim's kids.

3. Sue wants to go to Chinatown for dinner.

PRACTICE 1

Ask someone what he/she did this weekend.
Say what you did.

SUE: What did you do this weekend?
JIM: I went sightseeing with my kids.

A: What did you do ....?
B: ....

NOTE:

On Monday ask:
  What did you do **this** weekend?
On the other days ask:
  What did you do **last** weekend?

PRACTICE 2

Ask someone if he/she went somewhere.
Say where you went.

SUE: Did you go to the World Trade Center?
JIM: No, we went to get something to eat instead.

A: Did you go to ....?
B: No, I/we went to .... (instead). *or* Yes, I/we did.

PRACTICE 3

Ask someone if he's/she's been somewhere.
Say if you've been somewhere.

JIM: Have you been to the top of the World Trade Center?
SUE: Uh-huh. My husband and I went last year.

A: Have you been to ....?
B: Uh-huh. .... went .... *or* No, I haven't.

The World Trade Center

PRACTICE 4

Suggest going somewhere. Agree to go somewhere or say you can't go.

SUE: Why don't we go to the World Trade Center next weekend?
JIM: That's a good idea.

A: Why don't we .... next weekend/tonight/tomorrow?
B: That's a good idea. *or* I can't next weekend/tonight/tomorrow.

PRACTICE 5

Find the past tense of
go, do, walk, think, is,
are, meet, see, have, get,
make, win.

```
O C W E N T L A
L W A S Z H A D
M O L A G O T L
K N K W V U M S
D M E T K G M O
M A D I D H E R
G D E O M T L I
W E R E R U M O
```

PRACTICE 6

Open Conversation

A: What did you do ....?   B: ....
B: I went ....   A: Have you been to ....?
A: Did you ....?   B: ....

E X P A N S I O N

Welcome to

NEW YORK CITY

New York City has a population of nearly 10 million people. It is the largest city in the United States and the fourth largest city in the world. Only Shanghai, Tokyo and Mexico City are larger. New York City is one of the world's most important centers of business and culture. It is also the home of the United Nations. Here are some of the exciting places you can visit:

The Metropolitan Museum of Art, at 82nd Street and Fifth Avenue, is the largest art museum in the Western Hemisphere. It has works of art from all over the world. A new room has just been built for an ancient Egyptian temple.

_____, West of Broadway from 14th Street to Spring Street, is one of the oldest sections of New York. It has beautiful old houses where many famous artists and writers have lived. Washington Square, with its famous Washington Arch, is a well-known meeting place where people come to walk, talk or listen to street concerts.

_____, at Fifth Avenue and 34th Street, was the world's tallest building from 1931 until 1977. It has 102 floors and is 1,472 feet high. On a clear day you can see for 50 miles from the top floor. It's open from 9:30 AM until midnight every day.

_____ was a gift from France in 1886. It is on Liberty Island, south of Manhattan. Boats leave Battery Park hourly from 9 AM to 4 PM.

_____'s narrow streets, old buildings, shops and restaurants have been the center of New York's Chinese community for more than 100 years. It is a fascinating place to walk and have lunch or dinner.

The two towers of the _____ are now the tallest buildings in New York. Each tower has 112 floors. 50,000 people work in the two towers. At the top of the North Tower there is a restaurant and a bar with a beautiful view of Manhattan. There is an observation deck at the top of the South Tower.

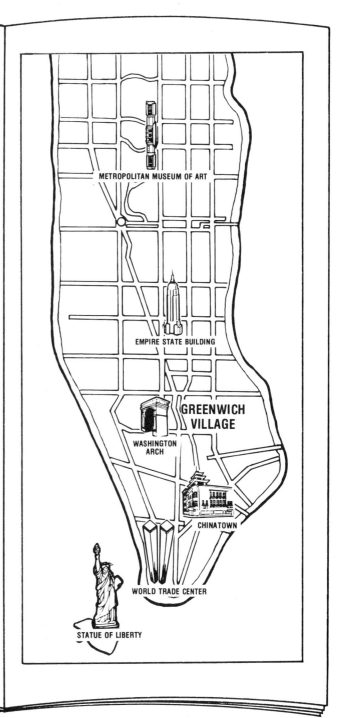

PRACTICE 7 Here's a page from a New York City guidebook.
Read each paragraph and look for the name of the place on the map.
Write the name in the blank.

PRACTICE 8

Read this post card from Tony to his parents. Then write your own post card.

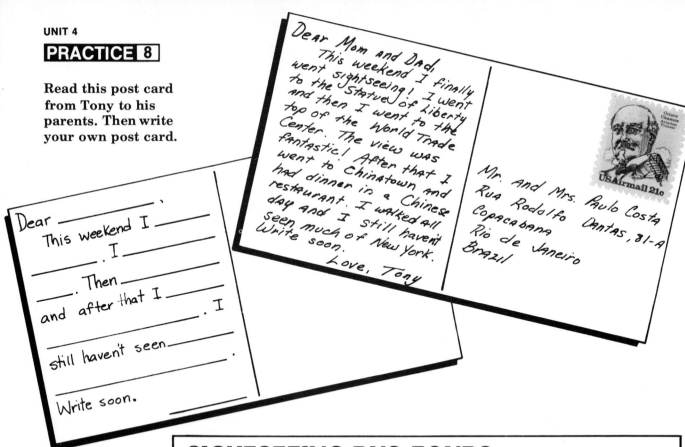

Dear Mom and Dad,
This weekend I finally went sightseeing! I went to the Statue of Liberty and then I went to the top of the World Trade Center. The view was fantastic! After that I went to Chinatown and had dinner in a Chinese restaurant. I walked all day and I still haven't seen much of New York. Write soon.
Love, Tony

Mr. and Mrs. Paulo Costa
Rua Rodolfo Dantas, 81-A
Copacabana
Rio de Janeiro
Brazil

Dear _____ ,
This weekend I _____
_____ . I _____
_____ . Then _____
_____ . and after that I _____
_____ . I _____
still haven't seen _____
_____ .
Write soon. _____

PRACTICE 9

Listen to the tour guide and look at the brochure. Circle the number of the tour he is talking about.

SIGHTSEEING BUS TOURS

TOUR 1 about 2½ hours **$6.50**

Midtown

10:00 A.M., 12:00 noon, 2:00 P.M.

Museums. Central Park. Fifth Avenue. Rockefeller Center. Times Square. United Nations.

TOUR 2 about 4 hours **$8.50**

Lower New York

10:00 A.M., 12:15 P.M., 2:15 P.M.

Times Square. Empire State Building. Greenwich Village. World Trade Center. Statue of Liberty. Chinatown.

HOW MUCH DO YOU KNOW?

1. Complete the Conversation

SUE: ....?

JIM: I went ....

SUE: ....?

JIM: No, but I'd like to go.

SUE: ....?

JIM: I can't. I have to ....

28

2. Find the Conversation

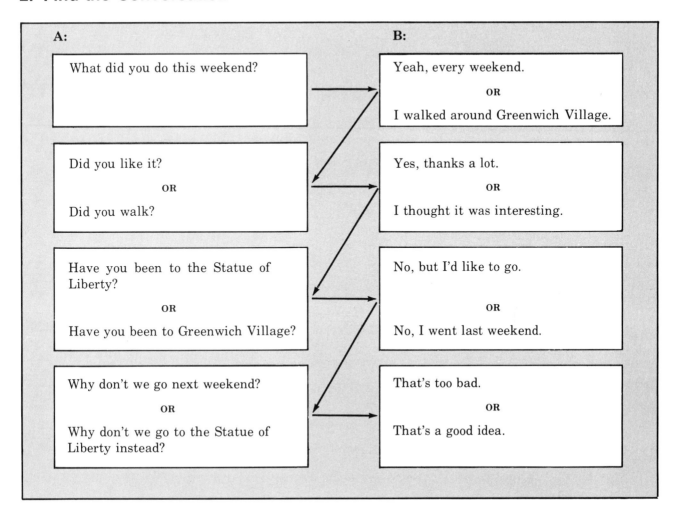

A:

> What did you do this weekend?

> Did you like it?
>
> OR
>
> Did you walk?

> Have you been to the Statue of Liberty?
>
> OR
>
> Have you been to Greenwich Village?

> Why don't we go next weekend?
>
> OR
>
> Why don't we go to the Statue of Liberty instead?

B:

> Yeah, every weekend.
>
> OR
>
> I walked around Greenwich Village.

> Yes, thanks a lot.
>
> OR
>
> I thought it was interesting.

> No, but I'd like to go.
>
> OR
>
> No, I went last weekend.

> That's too bad.
>
> OR
>
> That's a good idea.

3. Circle the Answer

1. A: ....
   a) What did you do? b) Why don't we go next Saturday? c) When?
   B: I went to the Metropolitan Museum.

2. A: ....
   a) Why don't you go to Greenwich Village? b) Did you go to Times Square?
   c) Did you stay home?
   B: I thought about going, but I went to Greenwich Village instead.

3. A: ....
   a) Have you been to Central Park? b) Let's go to Central Park.
   c) Why don't we go to Central Park?
   B: No, but I'd like to go.

4. A: ....
   a) Do you go to Chinatown very often? b) Why don't we go to the Statue of Liberty?
   c) Where did you go?
   B: I can't. I have to study.

LANGUAGE SUMMARY

Now You Can Do This:

talk about the past:	What did you do this weekend? I went sightseeing.
make a suggestion:	Why don't we go to the World Trade Center next weekend? Let's go to Chinatown.
accept a suggestion:	That's a good idea.
say you can't accept a suggestion:	I can't next weekend/tonight/tomorrow.

Grammar

Past Tense: Questions ⟶ And Answers

What	**did**	you	**do** this weekend?	**I went** sightseeing.
Where	**did**	you	**go?**	To the zoo.
	Did	you	**go** to Chinatown?	No.

Instead

Did you go to the World Trade Center?	No, I went to Chinatown **instead.**

Present Perfect: Questions ⟶ And Short Answers

Have you **been** to the World Trade Center?	No, I **haven't.** Yes, I **have.**

Useful Words and Expressions

haven't
•
walk
•
sightseeing
kids
top
•
next
•
instead

How do you like New York?

Tony's in the laundry room of his apartment building.
He's talking to Ruth when Grace comes in.

RUTH: So, how do you like New York, Tony?

TONY: Oh, I really like it. It's exciting and there's always something to do. But it's expensive.

RUTH: Mmmh. I like it here too. But you're right. It's expensive *and* dirty. It was so nice when I moved here twenty years ago.

TONY: You've been here for twenty years?

RUTH: Uh-huh. And in those days the streets were clean and you could walk in the park at night. But now the neighborhood isn't very safe. You know, Grace's apartment was robbed last week.

TONY: No! Really?

RUTH: Yes, they took her TV and . . . Oh, hi, Grace.

GRACE: Hello, Ruth. Hi, Tony. . . . Say, Ruth, I was just talking to Rose. She wants to join our bridge club. What do you think of her?

RUTH: I don't like her. I think she's selfish and rude.

GRACE: Oh, come on. Rose isn't so bad. She's a lot of fun.

RUTH: She's obnoxious and her husband's even worse. Do you know him?

GRACE: I don't think so. What does he look like?

RUTH: He's tall and fat, wears glasses and has a mustache.

GRACE: Oh, I know who you mean.

RUTH: Yeah, well, let me tell you what he did the other . . . Oh, hello, Rose. My, you look pretty. That's a beautiful dress.

ROSE: Oh, thank you.

Answer *That's right* **or** *That's wrong.*

1. Ruth likes Rose.

2. Grace likes Rose.

3. Rose likes Ruth's dress.

Talk about places and people like this:

How do you like ....?
What do you think of ....?

	nice.		nice.
	OK.		OK.
	all right.		all right.
It's	not so bad.	He's/She's/They're	not so bad.
	terrific.		terrific.
	crowded.		great.
	cheap.		terrible.
	awful.		awful.
	or		*or*
I've never been there.		I don't know him/her/them.	

PRACTICE 1   Ask what someone thinks about a place.
Say why you like or dislike a place.

RUTH: How do you like New York?
TONY: I really like it. There's always something to do. But it's expensive.
RUTH: I like it too.

A: How do you like ....? *or* What do you
     think of ....?
B: I like it. It's .... (But ....)
   or I don't like it. It's .... (But ....)
A: I like it too. *or* I don't like it either.

PRACTICE 2   Ask what someone thinks of another person.
Say what you think of another person.

GRACE: What do you think of Rose?
RUTH: I don't like her. I think she's selfish and rude.

A: What do you think of ....? *or* How do
     you like ....?
B: I like/don't like .... I think ....

PRACTICE 3   Fill in the blanks in this conversation with one of
the words in parentheses.

ROSE: Gee, Grace, Ruth told me your apartment was robbed. That's awful.
         Didn't anyone see who did it?
GRACE: Well, that new woman, Paula, said she saw a ...., ...
                                          (tall, short)   (fat, thin)
         man with a mustache near my apartment.
ROSE: Really?
GRACE: Uh-huh. She said he had ...., ... hair too.
                            (curly, straight)   (blond, black)
ROSE: Was it long or short?
GRACE: ...., I think.
     (Short, Long)
ROSE: That sounds like my husband! Was he wearing glasses?
GRACE: I don't know.

3A

PRACTICE 4 Say you don't know someone and ask what someone looks like. Describe someone.

RUTH: Do you know Rose's husband?
GRACE: I don't think so. What does he look like?
RUTH: He's tall and fat, wears glasses and has a mustache.

A: Do you know ....?
B: I don't think so. What does he/she look like?
A: ....

You can also say:		
He's medium height.		
He's about my height.		
He has	brown eyes.	
	long red hair.	
	short black hair.	
	curly blond hair.	

PRACTICE 5 Give someone a compliment. Accept a compliment.

RUTH: That's a beautiful dress.
ROSE: Oh, thank you.

A: That's a beautiful ....
B: Oh, thank you.

You can also say:		
That's a	nice very nice really nice	shirt. skirt. blouse. suit.
Those are		shoes. pants. stockings.

SHIRT
STOCKINGS
BLOUSE
PANTS
SKIRT
SUIT
SHOES
25¢
25¢

PRACTICE 6 Open Conversation

A: I like .... I think he's/she's ....
B: I ....
A: And do you know ....?
B: No. What does he/she look like?
A: He's/She's ....

EXPANSION

NEW YORK NEWS   WEDNESDAY, OCTOBER 24, 1979

Middle-Income Families Have Housing Problems

By William Hawthorn

Walter Lasky, Bob Edwards and David Thompson (not their real names) live in New York. Walter Lasky, head of a famous banking family, rents a nine-room apartment in the city and owns a house in the country. Bob Edwards, a bus driver, rents a three-bedroom apartment in a government housing project. David Thompson, a tax accountant, is not as wealthy as Walter Lasky, but he makes more money than Bob Edwards. Where does he live? David Thompson and his wife and daughter live in a one-bedroom apartment in an old building in a dangerous neighborhood.

"We've been looking for an apartment we can afford in a better neighborhood for over a year, but we haven't found anything," said Mr. Thompson. "Everything is too expensive."

A Common but Difficult Problem

The Thompsons have a common but difficult problem: they are not poor enough or rich enough to find a good place to live. People with low incomes like Mr. and Mrs. Edwards can find a place to live with help from the government. People like the Thompsons make too much money to get government help, but they cannot pay the high rent for a big apartment in a nice part of town. Even though they both have good jobs (Mrs. Thompson is a pharmacist) they live in an old, run-down apartment building in a dangerous neighborhood. If the Thompsons move to a better apartment, they will have to pay over half of their combined salaries in rent.

Since housing costs are increasing every year, the government is planning low-rent housing projects for middle-income families. However, it may be four or five years before these projects are finished. Until then, middle-income families like the Thompsons will probably have to stay where they are.

PRACTICE 7   Read the article and answer *That's right* or *That's wrong.*

1. The Thompsons are happy in the apartment they have now.

2. The Thompsons don't have the money they need to rent an apartment in a good neighborhood.

3. The Thompsons are poor.

4. Apartments in government housing projects are very expensive.

5. The Thompsons can get help from the government very soon.

PRACTICE 8   Circle the correct answers.

1. "We've been looking for an apartment we can afford" means

   a) the Thompsons are looking for an apartment they like.
   b) the Thompsons are looking for an apartment they can pay for.
   c) the Thompsons are looking for an apartment in a different neighborhood.

2. The Thompsons want to move to a better neighborhood because the neighborhood they live in is dangerous.

   a) A dangerous neighborhood has a lot of crime (robberies).
   b) A dangerous neighborhood is where rich people live.
   c) A dangerous neighborhood is in a nice part of town.

3. "They are not poor enough or rich enough to find a good place to live" in paragraph 3 means

   a) poor people can't find a place to live.
   b) rich people can't find a place to live.
   c) a middle-income family can't find a place to live.

4. In paragraph 4 *housing costs* means

   a) the money you pay for a house or an apartment.
   b) the money the government has to pay for housing projects.
   c) the money you pay to the government.

5. *Since* in *"Since* housing costs are increasing every year, the government is planning low-rent housing projects for middle-income families" means almost the same as

   a) because.
   b) until.
   c) but.

6. *However* in *"However,* it may be four or five years before these projects are started" means almost the same as

   a) but.
   b) for this reason.
   c) fortunately.

7. *Until then* in the last paragraph refers to

   a) in four or five years.
   b) low-rent housing.
   c) every year.

8. "Even though they both have good jobs, . . . they live in an old run-down apartment building in a dangerous neighborhood" means almost the same as

   a) they have good jobs, but they live in an old run-down apartment building in a dangerous neighborhood.
   b) they live in an old run-down apartment building in a dangerous neighborhood because they have good jobs.
   c) they don't have good jobs.

PRACTICE 9

This is Grace's letter to the landlord after her apartment was robbed. Look at the sentences in the box. Write the sentences that continue the idea of the letter.

> They took me to the movies.
>
> The robbers took my TV and my stereo.
>
> I saw a great movie on TV last night.
>
> It was about two robbers here in New York.
>
> They also took over $250.
>
> I have talked to the other people in the building and we have decided not to pay the rent until you make this building safer.
>
> My apartment is cold and you never fix anything.

October 19, 1979

Dear Mr. Davis:

There were seven robberies in our building last month, and I wrote to you saying the building was not safe. You didn't answer my letter and you didn't do anything. Now I'm writing to tell you that my apartment was robbed last night. _____

_____

_____.

Sincerely,

Grace Richards

(Mrs.) Grace Richards

PRACTICE 10

Listen to the six o'clock news. One of these pictures looks like the robber. Write *WANTED* under the right picture.

374629

875928

973142

297834

HOW MUCH DO YOU KNOW?

1. Complete the Conversation

TONY: ....?

RUTH: She's nice, but I don't like her husband. Do you know him?

TONY: No. ....?

RUTH: He's tall and fat, has dark hair and a big nose.

TONY: .... glasses?

RUTH: Uh-huh, and he has a mustache.

2. Find the Conversation

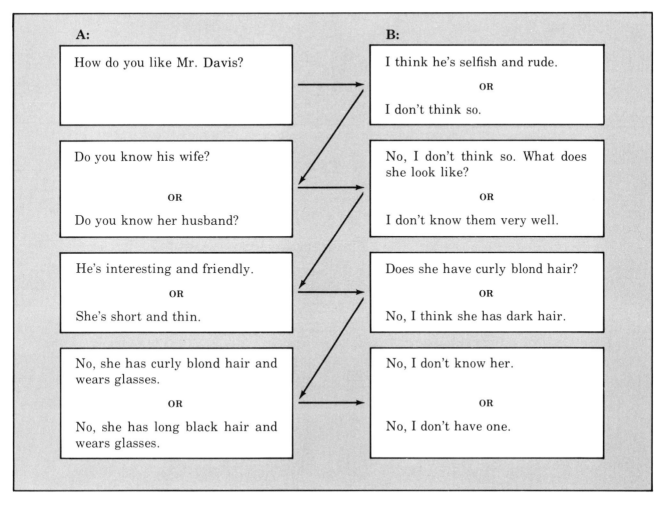

A:

How do you like Mr. Davis?

Do you know his wife?

OR

Do you know her husband?

He's interesting and friendly.

OR

She's short and thin.

No, she has curly blond hair and wears glasses.

OR

No, she has long black hair and wears glasses.

B:

I think he's selfish and rude.

OR

I don't think so.

No, I don't think so. What does she look like?

OR

I don't know them very well.

Does she have curly blond hair?

OR

No, I think she has dark hair.

No, I don't know her.

OR

No, I don't have one.

3. Circle the Answer

1. A: I really don't like New York.
    B: ....
    a) I don't like it either.   b) I like it too.
    c) I like them too.

2. A: I like Rose. I think she's nice.
    B: ....
    a) I like you too.   b) I like her too.   c) I like him too.

3. A: He's tall and thin.
    B: ....
    a) Yeah, and he wears glasses.   b) Yeah, and he's fat.
    c) Yeah, and he's short.

4. A: That's a beautiful sweater.
    B: ....
    a) That's nice.   b) That's OK.   c) Thank you.

5. A: I like Ruth's dress.
    B: ....
    a) Yes, it's a dress.   b) Yes, it's nice.   c) Yes, it's safe.

Policeman: *What did he look like?*
Woman: *Let's see . . . he had glasses, a big nose and a mustache.*

LANGUAGE SUMMARY

Now You Can Do This:

ask for and give an opinion:	How do you like New York? I really like it. It's exciting. What do you think of Rose? I like her. I think she's a lot of fun./ I don't like her. I think she's selfish and rude.
ask for and give descriptions:	What does he look like? He's tall and fat, wears glasses and has a mustache.
give and accept compliments:	That's a beautiful dress. Thank you.

Grammar

Too and Either

I like Rose.	I like her **too.**
I don't like Rose.	I don't like her **either.**

Adjectives

It's	**comfortable.**	
He's	**tall.**	
He has	**long blond**	hair.
She has a	**pretty**	dress.
That's a	**nice**	shirt.

Adverbs

That's a	**very**	nice coat.
That's a	**really**	nice coat.

Useful Words and Expressions

look like	shoes	short	rude
wear	skirt	medium	selfish
•	stockings	long	beautiful
glasses	suit	fat	pretty
mustache	dress	thin	•
hair	blouse	curly	always
eyes	•	black	either
height	those	blond	•
pants	•	brown	not so bad
shirt	tall	red	Mmmh.

I lost a sweater the other day.

A new tenant just came into the laundry room. Tony's talking to her.

PAULA: Excuse me, do you have a pen I can borrow?
TONY: Sure, here.
PAULA: Thanks. I need a desk and I thought I'd put a notice on the bulletin board.
TONY: You know, they have desks on sale at Macy's. I just saw an ad in the paper.
PAULA: Really? How much are they? I can't afford anything very expensive.
TONY: About $110.00, I think. Why don't you call and find out?
PAULA: That's a good idea. And do you know where I can get a bookcase?
TONY: I'm sure Macy's has bookcases too.
PAULA: All right. By the way, my name's Paula Duran. I just moved here from Chicago.
TONY: I'm Tony Costa. Welcome to New York.
GRACE: Come on, Ruth, let's go. See you later, Tony.

RUTH: Wait a minute. Just let me check the bulletin board. I lost a sweater the other day.
GRACE: Where did you lose it?
RUTH: I'm not sure, but I think I left it here in the laundry room.
GRACE: I found a sweater here the day before yesterday.
RUTH: You did? What does it look like?
GRACE: It's light blue with big buttons. Is it yours?
RUTH: No, mine's green.

Answer *That's right* **or** *That's wrong.*

1. Tony needs a desk and a bookcase.

2. Paula and Tony are good friends.

3. Grace found Ruth's sweater.

PRACTICE 1

Say what you need and ask how much it is.
Tell someone where he/she can get something and say how much it is.

PAULA: I need a desk.
TONY: They have desks on sale at Macy's.
PAULA: How much are they?
TONY: About $110.00 (a hundred and ten dollars).

A: I need a/some ....
B: They have .... at ....
A: How much are/is ....?
B: ....

> **NOTE:**
>
> a book   (some) books
> a bookcase   (some) bookcases
> a sweater   (some) sweaters
>
> **BUT:**
>
> (some) furniture
> (some) toothpaste

$ 0.50 (fifty cents)

$ 5.25 (five twenty-five/five dollars
        and twenty-five cents)

$25.99 (twenty-five ninety-nine/twenty-five
        dollars and ninety-nine cents)

PRACTICE 2

Read the *For Sale* notice.
Then write a notice for something you want to sell.

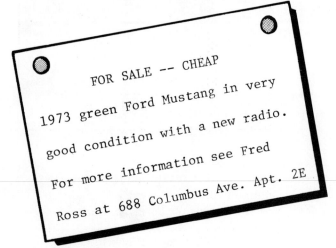

FOR SALE -- CHEAP

1973 green Ford Mustang in very

good condition with a new radio.

For more information see Fred

Ross at 688 Columbus Ave. Apt. 2E

```
            -FOR SALE-
    _____
        (what you are selling)
    _____
          (description)
see _____
              (name)
at  _____
            (address)
```

PRACTICE 3

Ask where you can get something.
Suggest where someone can get something.

PAULA: Do you know where I can get a bookcase?
TONY: I'm sure Macy's has bookcases.

A: Do you know where I can get a/some ....?
B: I'm sure .... has ....

> *You can also say:*
>
> Why don't you   call Macy's?
>   try Macy's?
>   put an ad in the newspaper?
>   look in the phone book?

PRACTICE 4   Say you found something. Ask someone to describe what he/she found.

GRACE: I found a sweater here the day before yesterday.
RUTH: You did? What does it look like?
GRACE: It's light blue with big buttons. Is it yours?
RUTH: No, mine's green.

A: I found ....
B: What does it/do they look like?
A: It's/They're .... Is it/Are they yours?
B: No, mine's/mine are .... or Yes, it is/
they are. or No, it isn't/they aren't.

NOTE:				
		black white		big/small buttons.
It's	(light/dark)	red yellow beige green blue gray	with/ and it has	long/short sleeves.
		checked plaid striped		a pocket/ a collar.

PRACTICE 5   Tell someone you lost something. Ask where someone lost something.

RUTH: I lost a sweater the other day.
GRACE: Where did you lose it?
RUTH: I'm not sure, but I think I left it in the laundry room.

A: I lost ....
B: Where did you lose ....?
A: ....

PRACTICE 6 Read the notice. Then write a notice for something you lost.

Last Wednesday I left a sweater in the laundry room. It's light blue with white buttons. If anyone has any information about it, please call Ruth at 872-9240.

NOTICE
_____ I lost/left
_____(in)_____.
It's / They're _____
_____. If anyone
has any information about
it/them, _____
_____.

PRACTICE 7 Complete the conversation with *him, her, it* or *them*.

RUTH: Say, Grace, where's my radio?
GRACE: I don't know. Where did you put ....?
RUTH: I put .... down with a couple of magazines, and now I can't find the magazines either.
GRACE: There's Tony. Why don't you ask ....?
RUTH: Well, he's talking to that woman. Who is she anyway? Do you know ....?
GRACE: Uh-huh. She's a new tenant. Oh, here are your things. Someone put .... on the floor near the washing machine..

PRACTICE 8

Open Conversation

A: I need ....
B: They have .... at ....
A: How much ....?
B: ....
A: And do you know where I can get ....?
B: ....

EXPANSION

Need ride to Livermore, Calif. (near San Francisco). Can help with expenses. Must leave before Jan. 5. Call 662-8494.

WILL SHARE TWO-BEDROOM APARTMENT WITH ANOTHER WOMAN. CAN PAY $200 A MONTH. SEE BETTY APT. 14E OR CALL 492-8764.

LOOKING FOR SOMEONE TO SHARE EXPENSES TO SAN FRANCISCO LEAVING JAN. 1 SEE CARL ANDERSON AT 688 COLUMBUS AVE. APT 19F OR CALL 333-3434.

WANTED - BICYCLE-10-SPEED ANY COLOR BUT MUST BE IN VERY GOOD CONDITION. 242-7000 OR SEE JIM IN 8D

Foreign student looking for American who wants to learn Spanish. Will exchange 4 hours of English conversation a week for 4 hours of Spanish conversation Call: Maria Sanchez at 886-9785.

I NEED A ROOMMATE FOR ONE-BEDROOM APARTMENT. ONLY $100 A MONTH. NON SMOKER, PLEASE AND NO PETS. CALL 492-8205 OR SEE JANE IN APT. 19C.

Young woman graduate student looking for a 1- or 2-bedroom apartment to share -Non-smoker. No cats. Call Debbie at 521-8883.

For Sale Red, 10-speed bike Almost new. Contact Tom in Apt. 24c

492-8205 492-8205 492-8205 492-8205

Looking for Spanish speaker who wants to exchange English for Spanish conversation classes. See Sylvia in 9F or call 492-8432.

PLEASE THINK OF OTHERS. DON'T SMOKE IN THE LAUNDRY ROOM

FOREIGN STUDENT NEEDS ENGLISH CONVERSATION PRACTICE. CAN PAY $5.00 AN HOUR. PREFERS YOUNG WOMAN. CALL ABDUL 492-7872

PRACTICE 9 Look at the notices on the bulletin board. In some of the notices people want something. In other notices people are offering something. Match the notices like the example above.

PRACTICE 10 Choose one of the notices on the bulletin board on page 43 as a model. Then write a notice for something you want or for something you have to offer.

_____
_____
_____
_____
_____

PRACTICE 11 Listen to the telephone conversation. Then choose the correct answers.

1. She's calling about

   a) a car.
   b) a bike.
   c) a radio.

2. It's

   a) two years old.
   b) four years old.
   c) six years old.

3. The man wants

   a) $14.00.
   b) $40.00.
   c) $44.00.

4. She can see it

   a) on Saturday.
   b) on Sunday.
   c) any time.

HOW MUCH DO YOU KNOW?

1. Complete the Conversation

RUTH: I lost a ....

GRACE: .... ?

RUTH: I think I left it here.

GRACE: I found one here the other day.

RUTH: What .... ?

GRACE: It's .... Is it yours?

RUTH: No, mine's ....

2. Find the Conversation

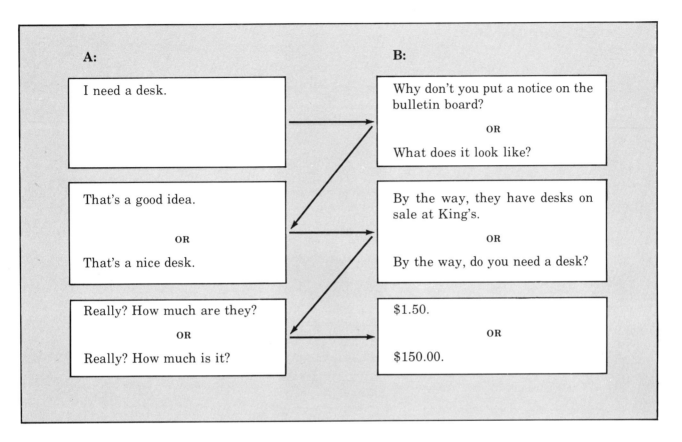

A:

I need a desk.

That's a good idea.

OR

That's a nice desk.

Really? How much are they?

OR

Really? How much is it?

B:

Why don't you put a notice on the bulletin board?

OR

What does it look like?

By the way, they have desks on sale at King's.

OR

By the way, do you need a desk?

$1.50.

OR

$150.00.

3. Circle the Answer

1. A: I need a bookcase.
   B: ....
       a) That's a nice bookcase.   b) How much is it?   c) They have bookcases at Korvette's.

2. A: How much are bookcases?
   B: ....
       a) I don't have one.   b) I have about $35.00.   c) About $100.00.

3. A: Do you know where I can get a TV?
   B: ....
       a) Why don't you look in the newspaper?   b) I don't know where it is.   c) Yes, I can.

4. A: I lost my sweater the other day.
   B: ....
       a) Maybe it's mine.   b) What does it look like?   c) I can't afford it.

5. A: I found a purse here yesterday.
   B: ....
       a) Is it yours?   b) Where did you find him?   c) Maybe it's mine.

6. A: What does she look like?
   B: ....
       a) She's friendly and interesting.   b) She's cold and tired.   c) She has blond hair and blue eyes.

LANGUAGE SUMMARY

Now You Can Do This:

say you need something:	I need a desk.
ask where you can get something:	Do you know where I can get a bookcase?
say where someone can get something:	They have desks on sale at Macy's.
make a suggestion:	Why don't you call Macy's?
talk about prices:	How much are they/is it? About $110.00.
talk about something you've lost or found:	I lost/found a sweater the other day. Where did you lose/find it?

Grammar

Word Order of Embedded Questions

	Where **can** I	get a bookcase?
Do you know where	I **can**	get a bookcase?

Possessive Pronouns

Is it	**mine?** **yours?** **his?** **hers?** **ours?** **theirs?**

Count Nouns

a book	(some) books
a bookcase	(some) bookcases
a sweater	(some) sweaters

Mass Nouns

(some) furniture
(some) toothpaste

Useful Words and Expressions

need	•	newspaper	yours	before
call	desk	sale	•	•
try	bookcase	dollars	light	yesterday
look	laundry room	phone book	blue	•
lose	bulletin board	day	green	on sale
found (find)	sweater	notice	big	By the way . . .
left (leave)	buttons	•	other	
put (put)	ad	mine	•	

Friends and Neighbors.

Paula's talking to Tony about living in New York.

HOW LONG HAVE YOU BEEN HERE, TONY?

FOR ABOUT THREE MONTHS.

PAULA: How long have you been here, Tony?
TONY: For about three months.
PAULA: Don't you miss Brazil?
TONY: Sometimes I miss my family, but living in another country's a fantastic experience.
PAULA: How do you like New York?
TONY: I think it's terrific. It's like a lot of small cities all together— Chinatown, Little Italy, Greenwich Village. . . . There's so much to do!

Answer *That's right* **or** *That's wrong.*

1. Tony has been in New York for two years.

2. Sometimes Tony misses his family.

3. Tony doesn't like New York.

PRACTICE 1   **Ask someone how long he/she has been here.**

PAULA: How long have you been here, Tony?
TONY: For about three months.

A: How long have you been here?
B: For/Since ....

PRACTICE 2   **Ask for and give opinions.**

PAULA: How do you like New York?
TONY: I think it's terrific.

A: How do you like ....?
B: I think ....

PRACTICE 3 Complete the conversation and practice it with a partner.

TONY: I went to Chinatown last Sunday.

PAULA: ....
1. How did you like him?
2. How did you like it?
3. How did you like her?

TONY: ....
1. I'd really like that.
2. I'd like to go.
3. I really enjoyed it.

PAULA: ....
1. Did you have a good time?
2. Did you have lunch there?
3. Did you have time?

TONY: ....
1. Yes, at the Peking Palace.
2. Yes, on Sunday.
3. Yes, in New York.

PAULA: ....
1. How are you?
2. How is it?
3. How was it?

TONY: ....
1. It was fantastic. Have you been there?
2. It was fantastic. Have you lived there?
3. It was fantastic. Have you studied there?

PAULA: ....
1. No, but I'd like something to drink.
2. No, but I'd like to stay home.
3. No, but I'd like to go sometime.

PRACTICE 4 Complete Tony's post card to his parents. Use some of these words.

park	write	fantastic	soon	to
city	see	cheap	before	
museum	hope	happy	on	
	miss	early	about	

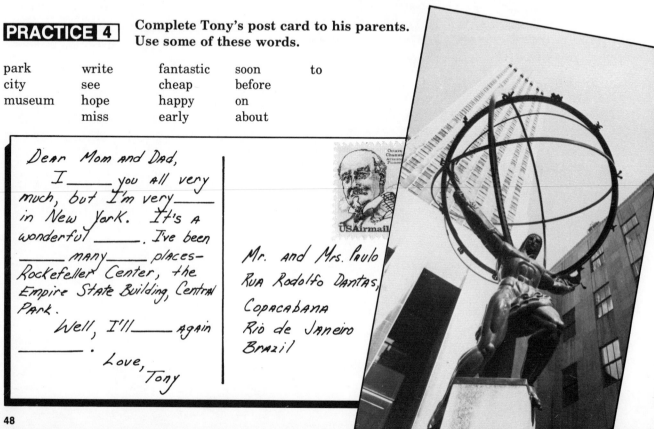

Dear Mom and Dad,
   I _____ you all very much, but I'm very _____ in New York. It's a wonderful _____. I've been _____ many _____ places— Rockefeller Center, the Empire State Building, Central Park.
   Well, I'll _____ again _____.
      Love,
         Tony

Mr. and Mrs. Paulo
Rua Rodolfo Dantas,
Copacabana
Rio de Janeiro
Brazil

PRACTICE 5   Read this page from a New York City guidebook and answer the questions.

Do you have a free day?

Two interesting areas to visit in New York are Chinatown and Little Italy. In both of these sections of the city people speak their native language and keep many of their customs. In Chinatown, signs, newspapers, books and even street names are in Chinese. There are markets where you can buy all kinds of Chinese food and, of course, there are hundreds of Chinese restaurants.

Nearby is Little Italy. You can visit interesting stores and markets here too. And don't miss the wonderful Italian restaurants. For a really special day, visit Chinatown on the Chinese New Year or Little Italy for a church holiday such as the Feast of San Gennaro.

Are the answers to these questions in the guidebook? Check (✔) Yes or No.

	Yes	No
1. Where's New York?	☐	☐
2. How many people live in Chinatown?	☐	☐
3. What are some things to see in Chinatown?	☐	☐
4. Where can you buy Chinese food?	☐	☐
5. When is a good time to visit Little Italy?	☐	☐
6. What's the name of a good Italian restaurant?	☐	☐

Tony and Paula are talking about what they did last weekend.

PAULA:	Do you like movies?
TONY:	Very much. Last Saturday I went to see *No Time for Love*.
PAULA:	How was it?
TONY:	Fantastic. I really enjoyed it. You shouldn't miss it.
PAULA:	Yeah, I've heard it's really good. I'll try to see it next weekend if I have time. I was so busy last weekend.
TONY:	Really? What did you do?
PAULA:	Well, I had to work all day Saturday, and in the evening I took some friends out to dinner. On Sunday I went to the Metropolitan Museum with them. Have you been there?
TONY:	No, but I'd like to go sometime.

Answer *That's right* **or** *That's wrong.*

1. Tony liked *No Time for Love*.

2. Paula wants to see *No Time for Love*.

3. Paula was busy all weekend.

PRACTICE 6   **Talk about what you did last weekend like this:**

TONY:	Last Saturday I went to see *No Time for Love*.
PAULA:	How was it?
TONY:	Fantastic.

A: ....
B: How was it?
A: ....

PRACTICE 7   **Talk about things you've done or seen.**

TONY:	What did you do last weekend?
PAULA:	I went to the Metropolitan Museum with some friends. Have you been there?
TONY:	No, but I'd like to go sometime.

A: What did you do ....?
B: I went to .... Have you been there?
A: ....

"Martha, where did you go?"

PRACTICE 8 Complete the conversation and practice it with a partner.

TONY: Did you have a nice weekend?

PAULA: ....
1. Yeah, I had breakfast.
2. Yeah, it was OK.
3. Yeah, I had a headache.

TONY: ....
1. What does he look like?
2. What do you do?
3. What did you do?

PAULA: ....
1. I went to bed.
2. I went sightseeing.
3. It was terrific.

TONY: ....
1. Where did you go?
2. Where were you?
3. Where is it?

PAULA: ....
1. To Central Park and the Metropolitan Museum.
2. On Fifth Avenue and 42nd Street.
3. In Greenwich Village near New York University.

PRACTICE 9 Complete this note from Paula to her friend Maggie MacDonald.
Use some of these words.

aspirin
Friday
movie
dinner
year
headache
boyfriend

talked
saw
said

could

expensive
good

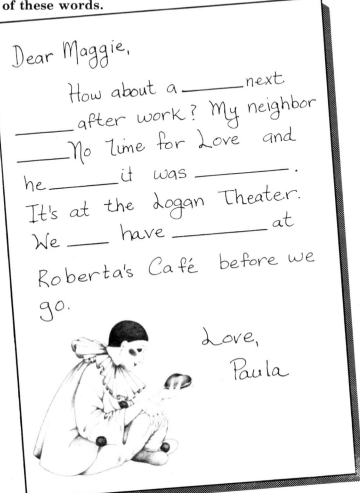

Dear Maggie,
   How about a _____next _____ after work? My neighbor _____ No Time for Love and he_____ it was _____. It's at the Logan Theater. We _____ have _____ at Roberta's Café before we go.

            Love,
            Paula

PETER MASTERS   GAYLE WYMAN

No Time For Love

with KATHLEEN TYLER and ARTHUR MANDEL

Music by Lydia Currie   Story by Nancy Fong   Produced by John Jarvis

Directed by Michael Croft

"A great movie you can't forget.—A beautiful love story. Don't miss it. . . . See it today."
—TERENCE TWEED

"*No Time for Love* has everything you want in a movie—music, mystery, excitement. . . . I loved it!"
—BEVERLY MOORE

G | General Audience

Logan Theater
Broadway & 46th Street
975-8386
11, 1, 3, 5, 7, 9, 11

Manhattan Embassy
72nd St. and 3rd Ave.
724-6639
12:20, 2:20, 4:20, 6:20, 8:20, 10:20

Answer *That's right* **or** *That's wrong.*

1. Beverly Moore didn't like the movie.

2. The movie is at five theaters.

3. *No Time for Love* is the name of the movie.

4. You can only see the movie at night.

5. Lydia Currie wrote the movie.

6. Terence Tweed thinks it's a love story.

7. *No Time for Love* is probably a science fiction movie.

PRACTICE 11   Do the crossword puzzle.

ACROSS

1. Man or boy.
2. Didn't win.
4. A number.
5. Let's go .... the movies.
7. A cold symptom.
9. The opposite of *come*.
10. He/She has a lot of students.
13. You go there when you're hungry.
15. 5 ACROSS.
17. A number.
18. I'm not ....
19. 17 ACROSS.
21. I don't like her. She's .... and rude.
23. The opposite of *small*.

DOWN

1. Where can I .... a bookcase?
3. You need one when it's cold.
4. A number.
6. There's a drugstore .... the corner.
7. You visit interesting places when you go ....
8. Not interesting.
11. Your father's or mother's sisters.
12. When you're hungry, you ....
14. Your father's or mother's brother.
16. A country in South America.
20. *I miss you* .... *Write soon*.
22. A pronoun.

Tony doesn't feel like going to class.

PAULA: What time is your English class?
TONY: At seven.
PAULA: It's 6:45 now.
TONY: I know, but I don't feel like going.
PAULA: Why not?
TONY: I don't feel very well.
PAULA: What's the matter?
TONY: I have a headache. Grace had a birthday party for her husband last night and it was so noisy I didn't sleep very well.
PAULA: Why don't you take a couple of aspirin?
TONY: No, I'll be OK. I just need to get some sleep.

Answer *That's right* **or** *That's wrong.*

1. Tony's class is at 6:45.

2. Tony's tired.

3. Tony doesn't want to go to his English class. He wants to sleep instead.

PRACTICE 12 **Say you don't want to do something and say why.**

TONY: I don't feel like going to class.
PAULA: Why not?
TONY: I don't feel well.

A: I don't feel like ....
B: Why not?
A: ....

PRACTICE 13 Talk about sickness like this:

PAULA: What's the matter?
TONY: I have a headache.
PAULA: Why don't you take a couple of aspirin?
TONY: No, I'll be OK. I just need to get some sleep.

A: What's the matter?
B: ....
A: Why don't you ....?
B: ....

PRACTICE 14 Complete the conversation and practice it with a partner.

TONY: Do you know Grace's husband?

PAULA: ....
1. I don't think so. What's her name?
2. I don't think so. What does she do?
3. I don't think so. What does he look like?

TONY: ....
1. He's very tall and wears glasses.
2. He's comfortable.
3. He's expensive.

PAULA: ....
1. Oh, yeah, I know that.
2. Oh, yeah, I know her.
3. Oh, yeah, I know him.

TONY: ....
1. What does he do? Do you know?
2. Who is he? Do you know?
3. What does she do? Do you know?

PAULA: ....
1. I think he's Grace's husband.
2. I think he's an electrician.
3. I think he's nice.

PRACTICE 15   Read "The Doctor Knows Best" and answer the questions.

The Doctor Knows Best

Dear Dr. Meritt: I'm a business student at New York University. I've always liked my classes and I usually get good grades—A's and B's. I'm active and healthy: I'm almost never sick. However, recently I've begun to get headaches—one almost every day. I never have them on weekends, but I get them about an hour before my classes begin. I saw a doctor, but he told me there was nothing wrong with me phys- ically. What's wrong? What can I do?

—Headache

Dear Headache: When did your headaches begin? Did you begin taking a different course? Have you had problems with a teacher or with your classmates? Is there a teacher or classmate you really like, or don't like? If there's nothing wrong with you physically, maybe your headaches are caused by something at school. Think about it.

Circle the correct answers.

1. The most important idea in the first paragraph
    is

    a) the writer is a good student and healthy.
    b) the writer is healthy, but she gets headaches
       before she goes to class.
    c) the writer likes her business courses, but she
       doesn't like her classmates.

2. The doctor thinks the student should

    a) talk to her classmates.
    b) stop thinking about the headaches.
    c) try to think about why she has headaches.

I'm having a party. Would you like to come?

Paula is inviting Tony to a party.

TONY: Oh, hi, Paula. How are you?

PAULA: Just fine. Listen, I'm having a housewarming party Saturday night. Would you like to come?

TONY: Sure. What time?

PAULA: Any time after eight. Here's an invitation.

TONY: Thank you. Do you mind if I bring a friend?

PAULA: No, not at all. Oh, and say, could I borrow your stereo?

TONY: Sure. Do you want me to bring some records too?

PAULA: Oh, that'd be nice.

TONY: OK. I'll bring everything over Saturday morning.

PAULA: OK. Thanks a lot.

Answer *That's right* **or** *That's wrong.*

1. Tony wants to go to the party.

2. Paula doesn't want Tony to bring a friend.

3. Tony is going to take some records to Paula's.

PRACTICE 1 Invite someone to a party. Accept an invitation and ask what time.

PAULA: I'm having a housewarming party Saturday night.
Would you like to come?
TONY: Sure. What time?
PAULA: Any time after eight.

A: I'm having a .... Would you like to come?
B: .... What time?
A: ....

> You can also say:
>
> I'm sorry, I can't.
> I already have plans.

Dinner Party

Cocktail Party

Birthday Party

PRACTICE 2 Ask for and give permission like this:

TONY: Do you mind if I bring a friend?
PAULA: No, not at all.

A: Do you mind if ....?
B: No, not at all.

PRACTICE 3 Ask if you can borrow something. Tell someone he/she can or can't borrow something.

PAULA: Could I borrow your stereo?
TONY: Sure.

A: Could I borrow ....?
B: Sure. or I'm sorry, I don't have one/any. or
I'm sorry. I need it/them.

PRACTICE 4 Offer to do something. Accept or refuse an offer.

TONY: Do you want me to bring some records?
PAULA: Oh, that'd be nice.

A: Do you want me to ....?
B: Oh, that'd be nice. *or* No, I don't think so.

NOTE: that'd = that would

You can also ask and answer:

Do you want me to bring anything?
Do you want me to bring anything else?
Yes, you could bring some Coke.
No, thanks.

PRACTICE 5 Complete the telephone conversation with *could, do, don't* or *does.*

PAULA:	Hello. .... I speak to Grace, please?
MR. RICHARDS:	Sure. Just a minute.
GRACE:	Hello?
PAULA:	Hi, Grace. This is Paula.
GRACE:	Oh, hi, Paula.
PAULA:	Listen, ... you have an ice bucket?
GRACE:	Uh-huh.
PAULA:	.... I borrow it Saturday night?
GRACE:	Of course. Oh no, wait. I forgot. I gave it to my daughter.

PAULA:	Oh. Well, ... Ruth have one?
GRACE:	I .... know, but I think she .... I'll ask her.
PAULA:	Thanks a lot.
GRACE:	.... you want me to bring anything else?
PAULA:	.... you bring some cups? I only have two or three.
GRACE:	Sure.

PRACTICE 6 Open Conversation

A: I'm having a party. ....?

B: .... What time?

A: ....

B: Do you mind if ....?

A: ....

B: Do you want me to ....?

A: ....

EXPANSION

October 25, 1979

Dear Mom and Dad,

I finally found an apartment and I moved in last weekend. It took me a month to find one that I liked and could afford. The one I found is kind of dark, but it's comfortable. The kitchen and bathroom are small, but the other rooms are big and I like the neighborhood. There's good transportation and there are a lot of stores and restaurants nearby. I think I'm going to like it here.

Everything is OK at work too. The hours are long and sometimes I have to work late, but the work is never boring and I'm learning a lot. I like the people I work with and they've been very helpful. As a matter of fact, I'm having a housewarming party Saturday and I've invited some people from the newspaper as well as some of my neighbors. It should be fun.

Well, I guess that's all for now. I still have a thousand things to do for the party. Say hello to everyone for me and tell them I'll write soon.

Love,
Paula

PRACTICE 7   Read Paula's letter and answer the questions.

1. Paula thinks her apartment is

   a) beautiful.
   b) terrible.
   c) OK.

2. Paula has been in New York

   a) all her life.
   b) two or three years.
   c) one or two months.

3. In the first paragraph Paula talks about

   a) her family.
   b) her job.
   c) her apartment.

4. In the second paragraph Paula talks about

   a) her work.
   b) her family.
   c) New York City.

PRACTICE 8 Read this note from Tony.
Then write a note to a friend.
Invite him/her to go somewhere with you.

Tomiko,
I tried to call you, but you weren't home. There's a party Saturday night at Paula Duran's, my new neighbor. I think it'll be fun. Would you like to go? It begins around 8:00. Why don't you call me later? I have to work tonight, but I'll be home around 10:00.
Tony

_____,

There's a _____.
I think it'll be _____.
Would you like to _____? It begins at _____. Why don't you _____?

_____

PRACTICE 9 Call and invite someone to a party. Accept an invitation and ask for information like this:

A: I'm having a .... Would you like to come?

B: Sure. What time?

A: At ....

B: What's your address?

A: ....

B: And what's your telephone number?

A: ....

PRACTICE 10

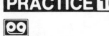

Tomiko's calling Tony, but she gets a recording. Listen to the recording. What was Tony's old number? What's his new number?

Tony's old number was ....

Tony's new number is ....

HOW MUCH DO YOU KNOW?

1. Complete the Conversation

PAULA:	I'm having a party next Saturday. Would you like to come?
A FRIEND:	....?
PAULA:	Any time after 8:00.
A FRIEND:	.... address?
PAULA:	....
A FRIEND:	.... telephone number?
PAULA:	....

"I'm having a dinner party. Would you like to come?"

2. Find the Conversation

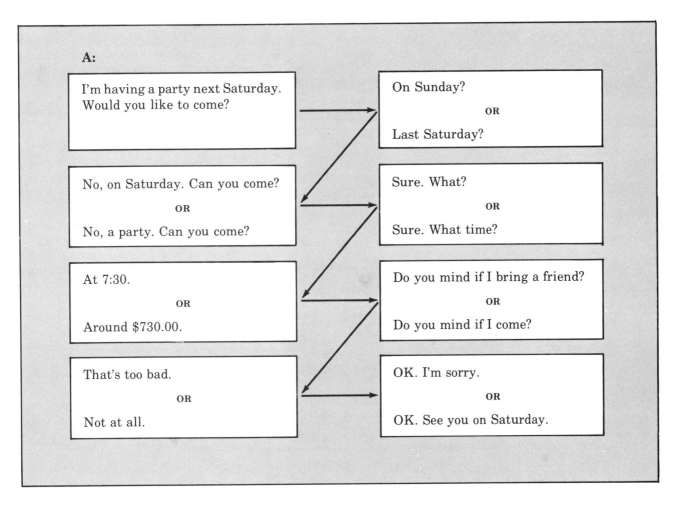

A:

I'm having a party next Saturday. Would you like to come?

On Sunday?

OR

Last Saturday?

No, on Saturday. Can you come?

OR

No, a party. Can you come?

Sure. What?

OR

Sure. What time?

At 7:30.

OR

Around $730.00.

Do you mind if I bring a friend?

OR

Do you mind if I come?

That's too bad.

OR

Not at all.

OK. I'm sorry.

OR

OK. See you on Saturday.

3. Circle the Answer

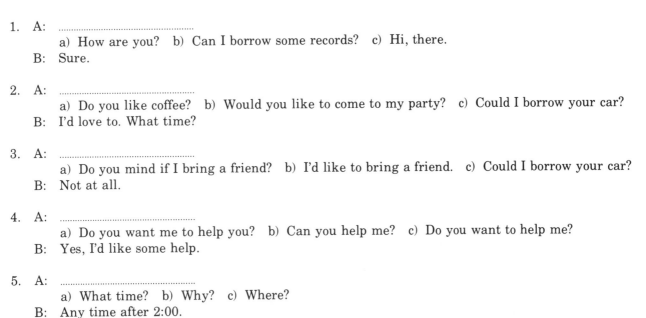

1. A: ....
   a) How are you?   b) Can I borrow some records?   c) Hi, there.
   B: Sure.

2. A: ....
   a) Do you like coffee?   b) Would you like to come to my party?   c) Could I borrow your car?
   B: I'd love to. What time?

3. A: ....
   a) Do you mind if I bring a friend?   b) I'd like to bring a friend.   c) Could I borrow your car?
   B: Not at all.

4. A: ....
   a) Do you want me to help you?   b) Can you help me?   c) Do you want to help me?
   B: Yes, I'd like some help.

5. A: ....
   a) What time?   b) Why?   c) Where?
   B: Any time after 2:00.

LANGUAGE SUMMARY

Now You Can Do This:

invite someone to do something:	I'm having a party tomorrow night. Would you like to come?
accept an invitation:	Sure.
ask and say what time:	What time? Any time after eight.
ask for and give permission:	Do you mind if I bring a friend? No, not at all.
make a request:	Could I borrow your stereo?
accept a request:	Sure.
refuse a request:	I'm sorry, I don't have one./I'm sorry, I need it.
offer to do something:	Do you want me to bring some records?
accept an offer:	That'd be nice.
refuse an offer:	No, I don't think so.

Grammar

Present Progressive as Future

> I'm **having** a party **tomorrow.**

Could and **Would**

Could I **borrow** some records? **Would** you **like** to come?	Sure.

Do you mind if + Present

Do you mind if I **bring** a friend?	No, not at all.

Want + Object Pronoun + Infinitive

Do you **want**	**me** **him** **her** **them** **us**	**to bring** anything?

Useful Words and Expressions

went (go)	records	Coke	housewarming	•	Do you mind if . . .
bring	stereo	night	else	after	Not at all.
borrow	party	•	•	•	That'd be nice.
come	plans	anything	already	if	
•	friend	•	any time	•	

How've you been?

Tony, Grace and Paula are talking at Paula's party.

GRACE: Well, Tony, how've you been?

TONY: Just fine, Mrs. Richards. And you?

GRACE: OK, I guess. . . . and please call me Grace.

PAULA: Would you like a cigarette, Grace?

GRACE: No, thank you. I don't smoke.

PAULA: Tony?

TONY: No, thanks.

PAULA: Tony told me you were robbed a couple of weeks ago.

GRACE: Yes. I get nervous every time I think about it.

PAULA: I know what you mean. I was robbed once in Chicago and it was a terrible experience. Can I get you anything?

GRACE: Do you have any orange juice?

PAULA: Sure. Oh, excuse me for a minute, there's the doorbell.

TONY: I'll get the orange juice. Where is it?

PAULA: On the kitchen counter.

TONY: Here's your orange juice, Grace. Oh, I'm sorry!

GRACE: That's OK. Don't worry about it. It's an old dress anyway.

TONY: Just a minute. I'll get a towel. I saw one in the kitchen.

Answer *That's right* **or** *That's wrong.*

1. Grace's last name is Richards.

2. The orange juice is in the refrigerator.

3. Tony is sorry that he spilled the orange juice on Grace's dress.

4. Paula and Grace were robbed two weeks ago.

PRACTICE 1   Greet someone like this:

GRACE: How've you been?
TONY: Just fine. And you?
GRACE: OK, I guess.

A: How've you been?
B: .... And you?
A: ....

> You can also say:
>
> Pretty good.
> Oh, not too bad.
> All right.

PRACTICE 2   Offer something to someone. Accept or refuse something.

PAULA: Would you like a cigarette?
GRACE: No, thank you. I don't smoke.

A: Would you like a ....?
B: No, thank you. ..../Yes, thank you.

> You can also answer:
>
> No, thank you. I don't drink.
> No, thank you. I'm not hungry/thirsty.
> Yes, please.

PRACTICE 3   Offer to get something for someone. Ask for something to eat or drink.

PAULA: Can I get you anything?
GRACE: Do you have any orange juice?
PAULA: Sure.

A: Can I get you ....?
B: Do you have any ....?
A: Sure./I'm sorry, I don't have any.

> NOTE:
>
> | | Do you have | **any** orange juice? |
> |----------|-------------|-----------------------|
> | I'm sorry, | I don't have | **any.** |
> | | I   have | **some** Coke. |

PRACTICE 4   Work with a partner and ask where things are.
(One person looks at the picture on page 67 and answers.)

TONY: Where's the orange juice?
PAULA: On the kitchen counter.

Ask where these things are:

sugar	knife
bread	orange juice
coffee	cat
tea	towel
glasses	milk
telephone	cheese
plates	apples
crackers	napkins

KEY

1 cabinet
2 stove
3 refrigerator
4 sink
5 counter

PRACTICE 5 | Look at the picture above and fill in the blanks with *in, on, next to, over* or *under*.

TONY: Where are the crackers?
PAULA: .... the cabinet .... the stove.
TONY: And the cheese?
PAULA: It's .... the refrigerator .... the milk.
The plates are .... the cabinet .... the
sink, and the napkins are .... the cabinet ....
the sink. I think there's a knife .... the counter.
TONY: OK.

PRACTICE 6 | Tell someone you're sorry you spilled/broke something like this:

A: Oh, I'm sorry!
B: That's OK. Don't worry about it.

You can also say:

That's all right. It doesn't matter.

PRACTICE 7 Open Conversation

A: How have you been?

B: .... And you?   A: Can I get you ....?

A: .... a cigarette?   B: Do you have any ....?

B: ....   A: ....

E X P A N S I O N

WHAT WOULD YOU DO?

Circle the letter that indicates how you would act in these social situations.

1. Your old roommate at college has just called you. You haven't seen each other for several years because he lives in another city now. He's in town for a very short time and you really want to see him. You have accepted an invitation to a dinner party and you want to take him to the dinner party with you.
   a) You call the host or hostess and ask, "Do you mind if I bring a friend?"
   b) You don't call the host or hostess but bring your friend anyway.
   c) You call the host or hostess and say, "I can't come if my friend doesn't come."

2. Your host or hostess has invited you for dinner at 8:00, but when you leave your office it's already 7:45. You hope you can get there by 8:00, but there is a lot of traffic and it's 8:30 when you finally arrive.
   a) You go home instead of going to the party.
   b) You go to the party and you don't say anything to the host or hostess.
   c) You apologize saying, "I'm really sorry. There was so much traffic I couldn't get here on time."

3. You are at a party and someone says hello. You are sure you know the person—but you can't remember his/her name.
   a) You say "I'm sorry, I've forgotten your name."
   b) You pretend that you've never met before.
   c) You don't answer him/her.

4. You are at a party and you are talking to a woman who accidentally spills her drink on you. She apologizes and
   a) you don't say anything.
   b) you spill your drink on her too.
   c) you say, "That's all right. Don't worry about it."

5. A friend sends you an invitation to a party and you can't go. Your friend doesn't have a telephone.
   a) You don't go to the party and the next time you see your friend you explain why.
   b) You write your friend a note and explain why you can't go to the party.
   c) You don't go to the party and pretend you didn't receive the invitation.

PRACTICE 8   Circle the correct answers.

1. In number (1) *several* probably means

 a) two years.
 b) more than two years.

2. In number (1) *a very short time* probably means

 a) two or three days.
 b) a month or more.

3. In number (1) *host or hostess* probably means

 a) the man or woman who invited you.
 b) your friend.

4. In number (2) *by 8:00* means

 a) at 8:00 or before.
 b) after 8:00.

5. In number (4) *accidentally spills* means

 a) the woman wanted to spill her drink.
 b) the woman didn't want to spill her drink.

PRACTICE 9

Dear Paula,
 Thank you very much for your invitation. George and I would love to come to your party, but we already have plans for Saturday night. It's our neighbors' anniversary and we've invited them over for dinner.
 I hope we can get together sometime soon. In fact, let's go to a movie next week. Thank you for thinking of us.
 Yours,
 Maggie

Paula also invited her friends Maggie and George MacDonald to her housewarming party, but they couldn't go. Read Maggie's note to Paula. Then write a note to a friend. Say you can't accept his/her invitation.

Dear _____,
 Thank you very much for your invitation. I'd/We'd love to _____ _____, but_____.
I/We/It's _____
_____.
 I hope we can get together soon. In fact, let's _____. Thank you
for _____.
 Yours, _____

69

PRACTICE 10

Tomiko has just arrived at Paula's party. She's late. Listen to the conversation and circle *True* or *False*.

1. Tony and Tomiko are talking about sports.　　T　　F

2. Tony has seen *Superman*.　　T　　F

PRACTICE 11　Tell someone you're sorry you're late and explain why like this:

A: I'm sorry I'm late. ....
B: Oh, that's all right.

> *You can say:*
>
> I couldn't get a bus/taxi.
> The traffic was awful.
> I had to work late.
> I couldn't find my car keys.
> My watch stopped.
> I got up late.

HOW MUCH DO YOU KNOW?

1. Complete the Conversation

GRACE: .... been?

TONY: Just fine, ...?

GRACE: .... anything?

TONY: Yes, I'd like ....

GRACE: Here it is. Oh, I'm terribly sorry!

TONY: ....

2. Find the Conversation

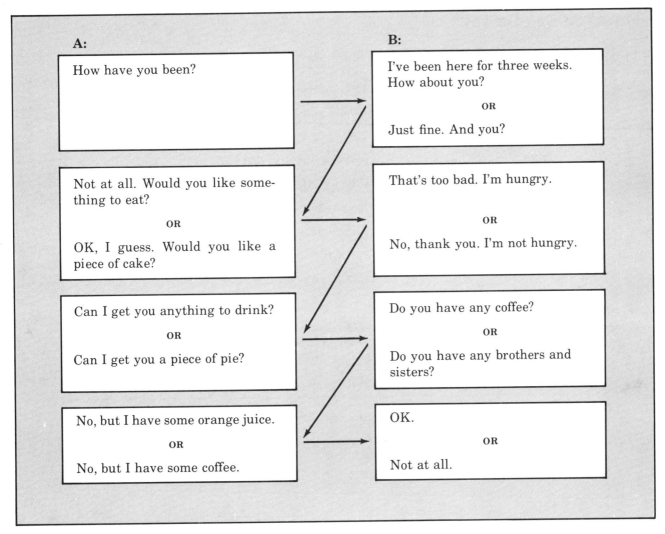

A:

How have you been?

Not at all. Would you like something to eat?

OR

OK, I guess. Would you like a piece of cake?

Can I get you anything to drink?

OR

Can I get you a piece of pie?

No, but I have some orange juice.

OR

No, but I have some coffee.

B:

I've been here for three weeks. How about you?

OR

Just fine. And you?

That's too bad. I'm hungry.

OR

No, thank you. I'm not hungry.

Do you have any coffee?

OR

Do you have any brothers and sisters?

OK.

OR

Not at all.

3. Circle the Answer

1. A: ....
   a) This is Tony Costa. b) How have you been? c) Excuse me.
   B: Fine, thank you.

2. A: ....
   a) Would you like a cigarette? b) Do you have a cigarette? c) What would you like?
   B: No, thank you.

3. A: ....
   a) Can I get you anything? b) Can you give this to Tony? c) Can you help me?
   B: Do you have any Coke?

4. A: ....
   a) Where's the coffee shop? b) Where's the restaurant? c) Where's the coffee?
   B: On the kitchen counter.

5. A: ....
   a) I'm sick. b) I'm really sorry. c) I'm very happy.
   B: That's all right. Don't worry about it.

LANGUAGE SUMMARY

Now You Can Do This:

start a conversation:	How have you been? Just fine. And you? OK, I guess.
offer something to someone:	Would you like a cigarette?
accept an offer:	Yes, thank you./Yes, please.
refuse an offer:	No, thank you. I don't smoke.
offer to get something for someone:	Can I get you anything?
make a request:	Do you have any orange juice?
accept/refuse a request:	Sure./I'm sorry. I don't have any orange juice.
apologize:	I'm sorry I'm late./Oh, I'm sorry!
accept an apology:	That's all right./Don't worry about it./It doesn't matter.

Grammar

Present Perfect: Questions ⟶ And Answers

How	**have** you **been?**	Just fine.
How long	**have** you **been** here?	About three months.
	Have you **been** to the World Trade Center?	No.

Anything/Any/Some

Can I	get you	**anything?**	No, thank you.
Do you	have	**any** orange juice?	I'm sorry. I don't have **any**
I'd	like	**some** orange juice.	(orange juice).

Prepositions

The coffee is	**in**	the cabinet.
	on	the counter.
	under	the counter.
	over	the stove.
	next to	the milk.

Useful Words and Expressions

couldn't	•	bread	bus	•
•	kitchen counter	tea	taxi	Don't worry about it.
smoke	refrigerator	cheese	car keys	It doesn't matter.
stop	cabinet	crackers	traffic	Pretty good.
drink	stove	plates	watch	Not too bad.
find	sink	knife	•	
worry	cigarette	napkins	late	
had to (have to)	orange juice	towel	hungry	
got up (get up)	sugar	cat	thirsty	

How do you get to work?

Tomiko and Paula are talking in the kitchen.

TOMIKO: Well, I hate to leave, but it's getting late and I have to work tomorrow.

PAULA: You work on Sundays?

TOMIKO: Not usually, but my boss asked me to come in tomorrow morning. He has an important meeting on Monday.

PAULA: Well, I'm sorry you have to go. What do you do anyway?

TOMIKO: I work for Japan Air Lines at Kennedy Airport.

PAULA: Really? That's pretty far from here. How do you get there? By subway?

TOMIKO: No, I take the bus.

PAULA: How long does it take you to get there?

TOMIKO: Oh, about an hour, but I don't mind. I usually read. What do *you* do, Paula?

PAULA: I'm a reporter. I work for the *New York News*.

TOMIKO: No kidding? I've thought about studying journalism. I'd like to talk to you about it sometime.

PAULA: Fine. Why don't we get together soon? What do you usually do on weekends?

TOMIKO: Nothing much. I always play tennis on Saturday morning, but my afternoons are free.

PAULA: Do you ever go to the ballet?

TOMIKO: No, not very often.

PAULA: Would you like to go next Saturday? I have two tickets.

TOMIKO: Oh, that sounds like fun.

Answer *That's right* **or** *That's wrong.*

1. Tomiko usually works on Sunday.

2. Tomiko doesn't like to take the bus.

3. Tomiko usually goes to the ballet on weekends.

4. Paula, Tony and Tomiko are going to the ballet on Saturday.

PRACTICE 1   Ask someone what his/her occupation is. Tell someone your occupation.

PAULA: What do you do?
TOMIKO: I work for Japan Air Lines.

A: What do you do?
B: ....

PRACTICE 2   Ask someone how he/she gets to work/school. Say how you get there.

PAULA: How do you get to work?
TOMIKO: I take the bus.

A: How do you get to ....?
B: I ....

You can say:

I take the bus/the train/the subway/a taxi.
I go by train/subway/bus.
I walk.
I drive.

I take the bus.
I go by bus.

I take the train.
I go by train.

I take the subway.
I go by subway.

I take a taxi.

I walk.

I drive.

PRACTICE 3   Ask and say how long it takes to go somewhere.

PAULA: How long does it take you to get to the airport?
TOMIKO: About an hour.

A: How long does it take (you) to ....?
B: (About) ....

NOTE:

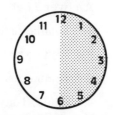

About 15 minutes.   About half an hour.

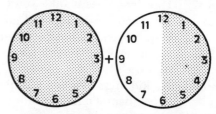

About an hour and a half.

PRACTICE 4 Ask someone what he/she usually does on weekends. Say what you do.

PAULA: What do you usually do on weekends?
TOMIKO: Nothing much. I always play tennis on
Saturday morning, but my afternoons are free.
PAULA: Do you ever go to the ballet?
TOMIKO: No, not very often.

A: What do you usually do on weekends?
B: ....
A: Do you ever .... ?
B: ....

You can say:
Yes, all the time.
Yes, sometimes.
No, not usually.
No, not very often.
No, almost never.
No, never.

PRACTICE 5 Look at the pictures and complete the conversation with
always, usually, sometimes **or** *never*.

TOMIKO: Your job with the *News* sounds exciting,
but I bet you're busy all the time.
PAULA: Yeah, during the week, but I ....
work on weekends.
TOMIKO: What do you usually do?
PAULA: Well, let me see. . . . On Saturday I
.... go shopping and have lunch
at a nice restaurant. And I ....
go to the movies on Saturday afternoon.
TOMIKO: And what do you do on Sunday?
PAULA: Well, I .... sleep late, and I

.... go swimming in the afternoon. I try to go to bed early because I
.... go to work early on Monday.

NOTE:		
always	100%	
usually		
sometimes		
never	0%	

75

PRACTICE 6 Open Conversation

A: What do you do?

B: ....

A: How do you get ....?

B: ....

A: How long ....?

B: ....

A: .... on weekends?

B: ....

A: Do you ever ....?

B: ....

E X P A N S I O N

Letters to the Editor

A PROUD NEW YORKER

(1) **To the editor:** I moved to New York City three years ago from a small town in Montana. My friends and family thought I was crazy. They said New

(5) York was a dirty, dangerous city. "Every time I pick up a newspaper I read about crime in New York," one friend told me.

I know there's a lot of crime here,

(10) but newspapers always make New York seem much more dangerous than it really is. They give the wrong impression of life in our city. Good news doesn't sell newspapers so all we

(15) read about is muggings and murders and disasters.

I'd like to tell you about another side of New York: the good side. Three weeks ago I broke my leg. The first

(20) week I couldn't walk. I live alone and I didn't have anyone to help me do things. During that first week my neighbors brought me food and went shopping for me when I needed some-

(25) thing. They were wonderful. Now I walk on crutches and everywhere I go

people ask me about my leg and try to help me. Bus drivers wait for me and people help me get on and off the bus.

(30) Complete strangers help me carry packages and get taxis for me.

These are the wonderful people in our city that you never read about and I'm proud to be one of them. It's true

(35) New York has its problems, but sometimes we need to think about the thousands of good people in our city. We might see one crime in a year, but how many times do people help us every

(40) day?

Richard Williams
New York City

PRACTICE 7 Read the newspaper article about New York on page 76 and circle the correct answers.

1. In line (15) *muggings* and *murders* are

   a) crimes.
   b) good news.
   c) newspaper articles.

2. In line (30) a *stranger* is probably

   a) a friend.
   b) a person you don't know.
   c) a helpful person.

3. In line (34) *proud* means

   a) the writer is happy he's a New Yorker.
   b) the writer isn't a New Yorker.
   c) the writer is sorry he's a New Yorker.

4. The main idea of the first paragraph is

   a) the writer doesn't like New York.
   b) the writer is from a small town.
   c) the writer's friends don't like New York.

5. The main idea of the second paragraph is

   a) newspapers never print good news.
   b) newspapers give us the wrong idea of life in New York.
   c) New York is a very dangerous city.

6. The main idea of the third paragraph is

   a) the writer broke his foot.
   b) people in New York are very helpful and friendly.
   c) the writer doesn't like to go to the grocery store.

7. The main idea of the fourth paragraph is

   a) New York has a lot of problems.
   b) the writer likes the people in New York.
   c) the people in New York have a lot of problems.

PRACTICE 8 Punctuate and capitalize the following newspaper article.

NOTE:	

Capitalize:
  Names of colleges.
  Names of hospitals.
  Names of streets.
	Put a comma before **but** like this:
	The assailant hit the woman with his gun, but he didn't shoot her.

Woman Mugged in Subway

last night a young woman from manhattan college was mugged by a man in the lexington avenue subway station the man hit her on the head and stole her purse at least four people saw the crime but no one helped her because the man had a gun the woman is in good condition at new york hospital the police are still looking for her assailant

PRACTICE 9

Tony's taking Tomiko home after Paula's party.
Listen to their conversation and answer *That's right* or *That's wrong*.

1. Tomiko likes the subway.

2. Tomiko can't hear Tony very well.

3. Tomiko invites Tony to a movie.

HOW MUCH DO YOU KNOW?

1. Complete the Conversation

PAULA: ....?

SALESMAN: I'm a salesman at Saks.

PAULA: ....?

SALESMAN: I take the bus.

PAULA: ....?

SALESMAN: About half an hour.

PAULA: ....?

SALESMAN: No. Never.

2. Find the Conversation

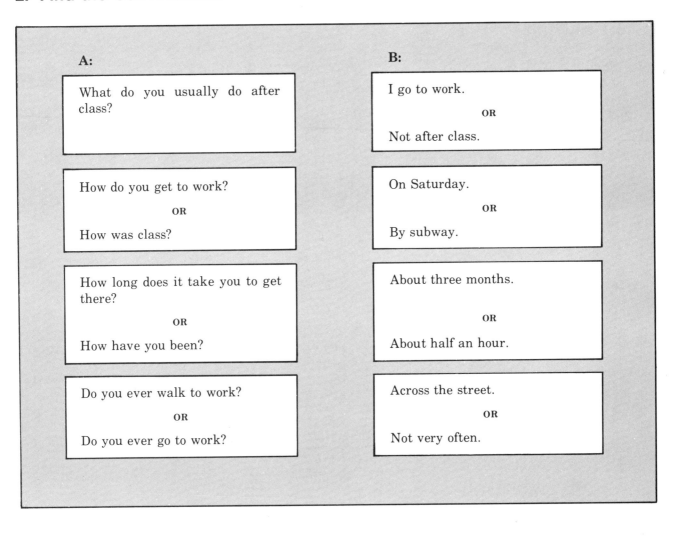

A:

What do you usually do after class?

How do you get to work?

OR

How was class?

How long does it take you to get there?

OR

How have you been?

Do you ever walk to work?

OR

Do you ever go to work?

B:

I go to work.

OR

Not after class.

On Saturday.

OR

By subway.

About three months.

OR

About half an hour.

Across the street.

OR

Not very often.

3. Circle the Answer

1. A: How do you get home?
   B: ....
      a) I never get home.   b) Not usually.   c) I usually take the subway.

2. A: How long does it take you to get to your office?
   B: ....
      a) How about you?   b) About an hour.   c) About 3:00.

3. A: Do you ever work on Saturday?
   B: ....
      a) I don't know.   b) Sometimes.   c) Yes, every day.

4. A: What do you usually do on Friday night?
   B: ....
      a) Yes, I do.   b) I get up early.   c) I stay home.

5. A: I often go shopping on Saturday.
   B: ....
      a) I'd like to go with you.   b) Would you like to come?   c) Sure, that sounds like fun.

LANGUAGE SUMMARY

Now You Can Do This:

talk about how to get places:

How do you get to work?
I take the bus./I go by train./I walk.

ask and say how long it takes to go
somewhere:

How long does it take you to get to the airport?
About half an hour./Not very long.

talk about what people usually do:

What do you usually do on weekends?
I always play tennis on Saturday morning,
but my afternoons are free.

Do you ever go to the ballet?
No, not very often.

Grammar

Frequency Adverbs

What do you **usually** do on weekends?	I	always usually often never	sleep late.
	I **sometimes** **Sometimes** I		sleep late.

Frequency Adverbs in Short Answers

Do you **ever** go to the ballet?	Yes, **all the time.** Yes, **sometimes.** No, **not usually.** No, **not very often.** No, **almost never.** No, **never.**

Useful Words and Expressions

drive	hour	by
walk	morning	•
•	afternoons	Nothing much.
ballet	half	Not very often.
airport	•	All the time.
subway	free	Not usually
train	•	Almost never.

Tomiko is talking to Tony on the phone.

TONY: Hello?

TOMIKO: Hello. Is Tony there?

TONY: This is Tony.

TOMIKO: Oh, hi, Tony. This is Tomiko.

TONY: Hi. What are you doing?

TOMIKO: I'm at the ballet. I'm waiting for Paula. Listen, what are you going to do later?

TONY: Nothing special. Why?

TOMIKO: Would you like to meet us for dinner?

TONY: Sure. What time? Oh, no, I forgot! I can't. I'm going to see *Superman* with Ali.

ERNESTO: Tony, could I see you for a minute?

TONY: Excuse me for a second. . . . What?

ERNESTO: Could I talk to you for a minute? It's important.

TONY: Sure. . . . I'm sorry. I have to go. My uncle wants to talk to me. I'll call you later, OK?

TOMIKO: OK. Bye-bye.

Answer *That's right* **or** *That's wrong.*

1. Tomiko's at home.

2. Tony's going to have dinner with Tomiko.

3. Tony's uncle wants to talk to Tomiko.

PRACTICE 1   Answer the telephone like this:

TONY: Hello?
TOMIKO: Hello. Is Tony there?
TONY: This is Tony.
TOMIKO: Hi, Tony. This is Tomiko.

A: Hello?
B: Hello. Is .... there?
A: This is ....
B: Hi, ... This is ....

PRACTICE 2   Ask someone what he/she is doing. Say what you're doing.

TONY: What are you doing?
TOMIKO: I'm waiting for Paula. What are *you* doing?
TONY: Nothing special.

A: What are you doing?
B: I'm .... What are *you* doing?
A: I'm ....

PRACTICE 3   Talk about the future.

TOMIKO: What are you going to do later?
TONY: I'm going to see *Superman* with Ali.

A: What are you going to do .... ?
B: I'm .... /Nothing special.

You can also say:
I don't have any plans.
I have to ....
I have a date (with ....).

PRACTICE 4   Invite someone to do something. Refuse an invitation.

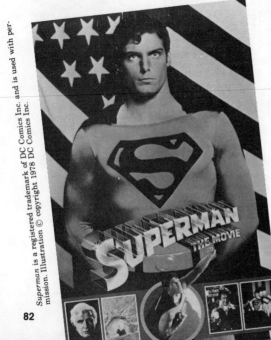

Superman is a registered trademark of DC Comics Inc. and is used with permission. Illustration © copyright 1978 DC Comics Inc.

TOMIKO: Would you like to meet us for dinner?
TONY: Sure. . . . Oh, no, I forgot. I can't.
           I'm going to see *Superman*
           with Ali.

A: Would you like to .... ?
B: Sure. . . . Oh, no, I forgot. I can't. I ....

You can also say:
I'm sorry, I can't. I ....
Thank you, but I can't. I ....

PRACTICE 5 Write Tony's part of the conversation.

(Tell Ernesto you're going to get a cup of coffee. Ask him if he'd like one.)

TONY: ....
....?

ERNESTO: No, thank you.

(Ask him what the matter is.)

TONY: ....?

ERNESTO: I just got a letter from the owner of this building. They're going to tear it down and I have to close the restaurant.

(Ask him what he's going to do.)

TONY: Gee, ...?

ERNESTO: Look for another place for a restaurant, I guess.

(Ask him if you can help him.)

TONY: ....?

ERNESTO: I don't think so. But I'm worried about you. What are you going to do?

(Tell him that you can get another job.)

TONY: Oh, don't worry about me. ....
....

PRACTICE 6 Open Conversation

A: Hello?

B: Hello, ... This is ....

A: Hi, ... What ....?

B: I'm .... What are *you* doing?

A: I'm ....

B: Listen, what are you going to ....?

A: I don't have any plans. Why?

B: Would you like to ....?

A: ....

EXPANSION

1 Listen for Dial Tone
2 Deposit 10¢
3 Dial Number

Emergencies—No coin needed

	Dial
Fire/Police/Ambulance	.911
Other Emergencies	"0"

No coin needed to Dial:	Dial
Directory assistance	.411
Operator assistance	"0" (Operator)
Repair service	.611

Different kinds of long distance calls

Person-to-person

Call person-to-person when you want to talk to a particular person. To dial a person-to-person call, dial operator + the area code + the local number. When the operator comes on the line, tell him/her you want to make a person-to-person call. The operator will ask you for the name of the person you want to speak to.

Station-to-station

Call station-to-station if you want to talk to anyone who

answers. To call station-to-station, dial the area code + the local number. Rates are lower for station-to-station calls than for person-to-person calls. If you're calling station-to-station, charges begin when someone answers the telephone.

Collect

You can call collect, either station-to-station or person-to-person, if the person you are calling will pay for the call. To dial a collect call, dial operator + the area code + the local number. When the operator comes on the line, tell him/her you want to make a collect call. He/She will ask you for your name.

PRACTICE 7 Read the page from the telephone directory and answer the questions.

1. Which is cheaper?

   a) A person-to-person call.
   b) A station-to-station call.

2. When you call collect, who pays for the call?

   a) You pay for the call.
   b) The person you call pays.

3. *The operator comes on the line* means he/she

   a) talks to you.
   b) stops talking to you.

4. A *coin* is

   a) money.
   b) a number.

5. In the number (212) 387-7876, the area code is

   a) 212.
   b) 387.

PRACTICE 8   Answer the phone and take a message like this:

A: Hello?

B: Hello. Is .... there?

A: I'm sorry. He/She .... Can I take a message?

B: Yes, would you please tell him/her .... called.

A: Sure.

B: Thank you.

A: You're welcome. Bye-bye.

B: Bye.

You can answer:
I'm sorry.   He's/She's busy right now. He's/She's sleeping. He/She isn't here.

PRACTICE 9   Listen to the telephone conversation. Then complete the message.

To ___Mr. Jefferson___

Date __10/30/79__ Time __1:30__   A.M. (P.M.)

WHILE YOU WERE OUT

M _____

of _____

Phone _____

TELEPHONED ☐   RETURNED YOUR CALL ☐

WILL CALL AGAIN ☐   PLEASE CALL ☐

Message _____

Will be in New
York on Tuesday
and would like
to see you.

_SD_

PRACTICE 10   Your boss is out. Someone calls and leaves a message. Write the message.

To _____

Date _____ Time _____ A.M.
                                                    P.M.

WHILE YOU WERE OUT

M _____

of _____

Phone _____

TELEPHONED ☐   RETURNED YOUR CALL ☐

WILL CALL AGAIN   PLEASE CALL

Message _____

_____

_____

_____

_____

HOW MUCH DO YOU KNOW?

1. Complete the Conversation

TOMIKO: ....?

TONY: I'm not doing anything special. Why?

TOMIKO: ....?

TONY: Sure. Oh, I forgot. I can't. I'm going to

....

TOMIKO: .... next Friday?

TONY: Next Friday's fine.

TOMIKO: OK. See you then.

WHAT ARE YOU DOING, JOE?

JUST GETTING SOMETHING TO EAT.

2. Find the Conversation

A:

> Is Tomiko there?

> Hi. What's that?
>
> OR
>
> Hi. What are you doing?

> Fine, thank you.
>
> OR
>
> Nothing special. Would you like to go to a movie tonight?

> Next week.
>
> OR
>
> The next movie is at 8:00.

B:

> This is Tomiko.
>
> OR
>
> Yes, she's there.

> I don't know. What are *you* doing?
>
> OR
>
> I'm watching TV. What are *you* doing?

> Sure, but I don't like sports.
>
> OR
>
> Sure, what time?

> All right.
>
> OR
>
> That's right.

3. Circle the Answer

1. A: Hello. Is Tony there?
   B: ....
      a) No, he's here. b) No, this isn't Tony. c) No, he isn't.

2. A: Hello, Tony. What are you doing?
   B: ....
      a) I study English. b) I'm a student. c) I'm studying.

3. A: What are you going to do next Saturday?
   B: ....
      a) I went to Boston. b) I go to Boston with my sister. c) I'm going to Boston.

4. A: Would you like to have dinner with me tomorrow?
   B: ....
      a) I'm sorry, I had dinner with my boss. b) I'm sorry, I haven't been there. c) I'm sorry, I'm going to have dinner with my boss.

5. A: I'm going to play tennis after class tomorrow.
   B: ....
      a) What about you? b) I'm going to go shopping. c) Would you like to play tennis?

LANGUAGE SUMMARY

Now You Can Do This:

start a telephone conversation:	Hello? Hello. Is Tony there? This is Tony. Hi, Tony. This is Tomiko.
offer to take a telephone message:	I'm sorry, he's busy right now. Can I take a message?
leave a telephone message:	Please tell him Tony called.
talk about the present:	What are you doing? Waiting for Paula. What are *you* doing? Nothing much.
talk about the future:	What are you going to do later? I'm going to see *Superman*.
invite someone to do something:	Would you like to meet us for dinner?
refuse an invitation:	I can't. I'm going to see *Superman* with Ali./ Thank you, but I can't.

Grammar

Present Progressive: Questions————➔And Answers

What **are** you What **is** he/she What **are** we/they	**doing?**	I'm He's/She's We're/They're	**waiting** for Paula.

Future Tense: **be going to** + base form

What **are** you **going to do** later?	I'm **going to see** *Superman*.

Useful Words and Expressions

sleep	dinner	•
wait for	date	later
call	message	•
listen	•	right now
tell	us	Nothing special.
forgot (forget)	•	Bye-bye.
•	busy	

What are you going to do?

Paula's on her way to get something to eat.
She invites Tony to go with her.

PAULA: Hi, Tony. I'm going to get something to eat.
Do you want to come?

TONY: No, I'm not hungry. Oh, on second thought,
I'll go with you. I want to talk to somebody.

PAULA: You look worried. Is anything wrong?

TONY: I lost my job. My uncle has to close the
restaurant because they're going to tear
down the building.

PAULA: Gee, that's too bad. What's he going to do?

TONY: Look for another place for a restaurant.

PAULA: What about you? What are *you* going to do?

TONY: Well, I'm looking for another job. I called
about one this morning, but it was already
taken.

PAULA: What kind of job are you looking for?

TONY: Anything, really, but I don't have any
experience except working in restaurants. I
don't know what I'm going to do if I don't
find a job.

PAULA: Oh, come on, Tony. It can't be that bad!
How long have you been looking?

TONY: For about a week.

PAULA: Well, I'm sure you'll find something.

TONY: I hope so.

Answer *That's right* **or** *That's wrong*.

1. Tony wants to get something to eat.

2. Tony wants to talk to somebody because he's
   worried.

3. Tony's uncle's looking for a job.

4. Tony's been looking for a job for three weeks.

PRACTICE 1   Invite someone to do something. Accept or refuse an invitation.

PAULA: I'm going to get something to eat.
          Do you want to come?
TONY: No, I'm not hungry.

A: I'm going to ....
     Do you want to come?
B: ....

> **You can also say:**
>
> Sure.
> That sounds like a good idea.
> No, thank you. I just ate.

PRACTICE 2   Ask if something is wrong. Tell someone about a problem.

PAULA: You look worried. Is anything wrong?
TONY: I lost my job.
PAULA: Gee, that's too bad.

A: You look worried. Is anything wrong?
B: ....
A: (Gee,) that's too bad.

> **You can also say:**
>
> I'm sorry to hear that.

"Is anything wrong?"

PRACTICE 3   Say you're looking for something and say what kind.

TONY: I'm looking for a job.
PAULA: What kind of job are you looking for?
TONY: Anything, really.

A: I'm looking for ....
B: What kind of .... are you looking for?
A: ....

> **If you're looking for a job,
> you can also say:**
>
> I'd like a job as a waitress.
> I'd like to work in a bank/office/hospital.

PRACTICE 4   Ask someone how long he/she has been doing something.
Say how long you've been doing something.

PAULA: How long have you been looking for a job?
TONY: For about a week.

A: How long have you been ....?
B: ....

PRACTICE 5

Tomiko and Tony are talking on the phone.
Write *where, what kind of, what, what time* **or** *how.*

TONY: Hello?
TOMIKO: Hi, Tony. .... are you?
TONY: Fine.
TOMIKO: I called before, but you weren't home.
TONY: .... did you call?
TOMIKO: About an hour ago. .... were you?
TONY: I went to get a newspaper. I'm looking for a job.
TOMIKO: .... job are you looking for?
TONY: Oh, anything, really. Say, do you want to go to a movie after class tonight?
TOMIKO: .... movie do you want to see?
TONY: *Everybody Dance.*
TOMIKO: .... is it playing?
TONY: At Cinema One.
TOMIKO: All right. See you in class.

PRACTICE 6   Open Conversation

A: You look worried. ....?

B: I'm looking for ....

A: What kind of ....?

B: ....

A: How long ....?

B: ....

E X P A N S I O N

STATE EMPLOYMENT AGENCY

Looking for a job: general hints.

1. Look neat when you apply for a job.

2. Fill out application forms neatly and completely.

3. Apply for the kind of work you know you can do well. During your interview talk about why you can do the work well and why you are interested in the job.

4. Don't be late for your interview.

5. Don't take friends or relatives with you.

6. Smile and be friendly. Don't go on a day when you are worried or depressed.

7. Don't talk about your personal problems or money problems.

PRACTICE 7   **Read the general hints on looking for a job and answer the questions.**

1. *Hints* are probably

   a) questions.
   b) suggestions.
   c) jobs.

2. *Neat* probably means

   a) good.
   b) bad.
   c) dirty.

3. *Fill out application forms completely* means

   a) fill out only the important things on the form.
   b) fill out everything on the form.

4. An *interview* is

   a) a letter to an employer.
   b) a meeting with an employer.
   c) a phone call to an employer.

5. When you're *depressed* or *worried*,

   a) you have problems.
   b) you don't have problems.

PRACTICE 8

Look at Tony's application form. Then fill out an application form for yourself. See the key if you have any questions.

A. PRINT LAST NAME — Costa	FIRST — Antonio	INITIAL	C. TELEPHONE NO. 373-6105	D. U.S. CITIZEN __ YES ✓ NO
B. STREET ADDRESS 688 Columbus Avenue Apt. 3F			E. DRIVER'S LICENSE __ YES ✓ NO	F. KIND OF WORK WANTED Cook, waiter, cashier
CITY NEW YORK	STATE N.Y.	ZIP CODE 10025		

G. EDUCATIONAL RECORD NAME AND LOCATION OF SCHOOL	DATES FROM	TO	MAJOR AND DEGREE
ELEMENTARY SCHOOL Dom Pedro II Rio de Janeiro, Brazil	2/65	12/70	
HIGH SCHOOL Escola Estadual Caetano de Campos, Rio de Janeiro, Brazil	2/71	12/78	
COLLEGE Universidade do Rio de Janeiro, Brazil	3/79	6/79	Business
OTHER American Language Institute New York University, New York, N.Y.	8/79	Present	

H. EMPLOYMENT HISTORY	
EMPLOYER Brazilia Restaurant	JOB DESCRIPTION Waiter and Cashier
CITY AND STATE WHERE EMPLOYED New York, N.Y.	
FROM 8/79 TO present SALARY 2.90/hr.	REASON FOR LEAVING restaurant closed
EMPLOYER Paulo Costa	JOB DESCRIPTION Waiter, Cashier and restaurant manager—part time
CITY AND STATE WHERE EMPLOYED Rio de Janeiro, Brazil	
FROM 1977 TO 1979 SALARY $100/week	REASON FOR LEAVING to study in U.S.A.

KEY
A. Print = *Costa* not *Costa*
B. Zip Code = Post Office Code

G. EDUCATIONAL RECORD
Major = what you studied at the university (business, architecture, medicine, etc.)
B.A. = the degree you get when you finish college
M.A. = the degree after B.A.
Ph.D. = the highest degree (Dr.)
From = when you started studying: month/year
To = when you finished studying: month/year

H. EMPLOYMENT HISTORY
Salary = how much money you made
Reason for leaving = why you left the job

A. PRINT: LAST NAME	FIRST	INITIAL	C. TELEPHONE NO.	D. U.S. CITIZEN __ YES __ NO
B. STREET ADDRESS			E. DRIVER'S LICENSE __ YES __ NO	F. KIND OF WORK WANTED
CITY	STATE	ZIP CODE		

G. EDUCATIONAL RECORD NAME AND LOCATION OF SCHOOL	DATES FROM	TO	MAJOR AND DEGREE
ELEMENTARY SCHOOL:			
HIGH SCHOOL:			
COLLEGE:			
OTHER:			

H. EMPLOYMENT HISTORY	
EMPLOYER	JOB DESCRIPTION
CITY AND STATE WHERE EMPLOYED	
FROM: TO: SALARY:	REASON FOR LEAVING:
EMPLOYER	JOB DESCRIPTION
CITY AND STATE WHERE EMPLOYED	
FROM: TO: SALARY:	REASON FOR LEAVING:

PRACTICE 9

**Listen to Grace's conversation with Tony.
What's she describing? Circle *a* or *b*.**

a) A job as a secretary for Tony.

b) A TV program.

HOW MUCH DO YOU KNOW?

1. Complete the Conversation

TONY: You look .... Is ....?

PAULA: No. Everything's fine. Say, I'm going to get
something to eat. ....?

TONY: Sure. Where .... going?

PAULA: ....

2. Find the Conversation

A:

You look worried. Is anything wrong?

That's too bad. How about you?

OR

That's too bad. What's he going to do?

What kind of job is he going to look for?

OR

What kind of job does he have?

Why doesn't he look in the newspaper?

OR

Why doesn't he look in his apartment?

B:

Yes, Mr. Johnson likes his apartment.

OR

Yes, Mr. Johnson lost his job.

Look for it.

OR

Look for another one.

That's a good job.

OR

A job as an electrician.

That's a good idea.

OR

That's right.

3. Circle the Answer

1. A: I'm going to get a cup of coffee.
    B: ....
    a) Do you want to come? b) Where? c) I'm not hungry.

2. A: Do you want to come with me?
    B: ....
    a) That's too bad. b) That sounds like a good idea. c) That's right.

3. A: Is anything wrong?
    B: ....
    a) I'm sick. b) I'm an accountant. c) I'm from Brazil.

4. A: I'd like to buy something to read.
    B: ....
    a) What kind of car are you looking for? b) What kind of TV are you looking for? c) What kind of book are you looking for?

5. A: How long have you been studying here?
    B: ....
    a) On 14th Street near the Olympia Theater. b) For about a year. c) Last month.

LANGUAGE SUMMARY

Now You Can Do This:

invite someone to do something:	I'm going to get something to eat. Do you want to come?
accept an invitation:	Sure./That sounds like a good idea.
refuse an invitation:	No, I'm not hungry./No, thank you. I just ate.
talk about problems:	You look worried. Is anything wrong? I lost my job.
sympathize:	That's too bad./I'm sorry to hear that.
ask and say how long:	How long have you been looking for a job? For about a week.

Grammar

Something/Anything

I'm going to get	**something**	to eat.
Do you want	**anything**	to eat?
Is	**anything**	wrong?

Present Perfect Progressive

How long **have** you **been looking** for a job?	I've **been looking** for a job for about a week.

Question Words

What time	did you call?	About an hour ago.
What movie	do you want to see?	*Everybody Dance.*
How	are you?	Fine.
Where	were you?	I went to get a newspaper.
What kind of job	are you looking for?	Anything, really.

Useful Words and Expressions

look for	electrician	•
hear	office	as
eat	hospital	•
•	•	That sounds like a good idea.
job	worried	Anything, really.
waitress	another	

UNIT 12 Why don't you get a roommate?

Tony's talking to Ali in the University Library.

ALI: Listen, how about going to the Jets' game with me tonight?

TONY: Thanks, but I don't feel like going out tonight.

ALI: No? What's the matter?

TONY: Oh. . . . I'm just depressed. I still haven't found a job, and I'm going to have to move. . . .

ALI: What do you mean move?

TONY: I can't afford my apartment anymore.

ALI: So, why don't you get a roommate?

TONY: Hmmm, that's not a bad idea. I could put a notice on the bulletin board at school.

ALI: Or better yet, you could put an ad in the *New York News.*

TONY: Yeah. Do you know where the *News* is?

ALI: Uh-huh. It's on the corner of 38th Street and Sixth Avenue.

TONY: How do I get there?

ALI: Take the subway to 42nd Street and you can walk from there.

Answer *That's right* **or** *That's wrong.*

1. Ali's depressed.

2. Tony wants to move to a new apartment.

3. Ali wants to be Tony's roommate.

4. Tony wants to get a roommate.

PRACTICE 1 Ask and say what's wrong.

ALI: What's the matter?

TONY: Oh, I'm just depressed. I still haven't found a job, and I'm going to have to move.

A: What's the matter?

B: ....

> *You can also say:*
>
> Nothing.
> I'm just tired.
> I'm worried. My father's sick.
> I'm in a bad mood. I had a fight with ....

PRACTICE 2 Make a suggestion. Accept or reject a suggestion.

ALI: Why don't you get a roommate?

TONY: Hmmm, that's not a bad idea.

A: Why don't you ....?

B: That's ..../No, I don't want to.

PRACTICE 3 Ask where something is. Say where something is.

TONY: Do you know where the *New York News* is?

ALI: It's on the corner of 38th Street and Sixth Avenue.

A: Do you know where ....?

B: It's ....

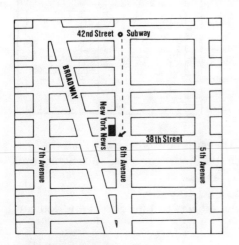

PRACTICE 4 Ask how to get somewhere. Say how to get somewhere.

TONY: How do I get to the *New York News?*

ALI: Take the subway to 42nd Street and you can walk from there.

A: How do I get to ....?

B: ....

> *You can also say:*
>
> Take the bus on Broadway and get off at 42nd Street.

98

PRACTICE 5   Write Tony's part of the conversation.

(Ask the man how you get to Sixth Avenue.)

TONY: Excuse me, ...
....?

MAN: It's right there.

(Ask if the man knows where the *New York News* is.)

TONY: ....?

MAN: Uh-huh, it's in that building on the corner.

(Thank the man.)

TONY: ....

MAN: You're welcome.

PRACTICE 6   Open Conversation

A: Hi, ...?

B: Not very well.

A: ....?

B: I'm depressed. I ....

A: Why don't you ....?

B: ....

EXPANSION

November 3, 1979

Dear Tony,

Your last letter was so depressing. I hope things are better now. It's really too bad that Ernesto had to close the restaurant, but maybe he'll find another place soon. Have you found another job yet? Do you have enough money? Maybe we can help you a little.

You asked about your father. I'm afraid he isn't any better. The doctor told him to stay in bed, but you know your father— he went to work two days later. I'm worried, but I don't know what to do.

I have to go now. Your father has a doctor's appointment at 4:30 and I'm going to go with him. I'm sorry I can't write a more optimistic letter, but I guess we all have our problems.

Please take care of yourself and give Ernesto our love.

Love,
Mom

PRACTICE 7 Read the letter from Tony's mother on page 100 and then circle the correct answers.

1. *I hope things are better now* means

   a) I want things to be better.
   b) I think things are better now.

2. *Do you have enough money?* probably means

   a) do you have a lot of money?
   b) do you have the money you need to live?

3. *We can help you a little* means

   a) we can help you find a job.
   b) we can give you some money.

4. *You asked about your father* means

   a) Tony asked his father for some money.
   b) Tony wrote his mother and asked if his father was OK.

5. When Tony's mother says *but you know your father,* she probably means

   a) Tony's father doesn't do what the doctor says.
   b) Tony's father always does what the doctor says.

6. *I just don't know what to do* means

   a) Tony's mother doesn't know how to help Tony.
   b) Tony's mother doesn't know how to help her husband.

PRACTICE 8 Look at Tony's ad for a roommate. Write an ad for a roommate.

WANTED
A male roommate for 2-bdrm.
Apartment on Columbus Ave.
near Central Park. Pref.
student. Must be responsible,
neat and quiet. Non-smoker, please.
Call Tony 373-6105

WANTED
_____
_____
_____
_____
_____
_____

NOTE:

bdrm. = bedroom
pref. = prefer

PRACTICE 9 Tony's calling his mother in Brazil. Listen and circle *True* or *False*.

1. Tony goes home to visit his parents. T F
2. Tony's father is sick. T F
3. Tony's mother is looking for a job. T F
4. Tony's father is a doctor. T F

HOW MUCH DO YOU KNOW?

1. Complete the Conversation

TOMIKO: ....?

PAULA: OK. I guess.

TOMIKO: ....?

PAULA: Oh, I'm just depressed. I don't feel very well and I have a lot of work.

TOMIKO: ....?

PAULA: I can't. I have to work. But call me later, OK?

TOMIKO: ....

2. Find the Conversation

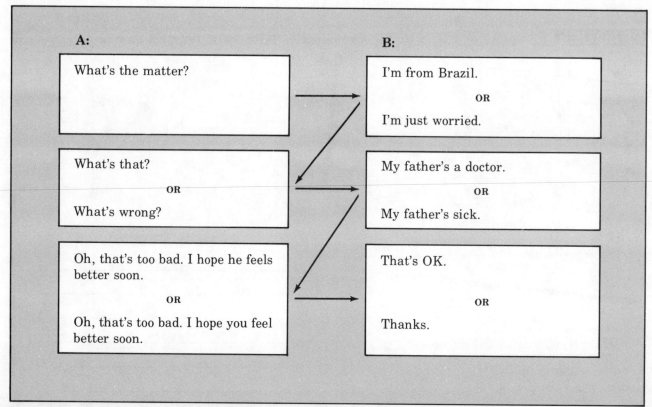

A:

What's the matter?

What's that?
OR
What's wrong?

Oh, that's too bad. I hope he feels better soon.
OR
Oh, that's too bad. I hope you feel better soon.

B:

I'm from Brazil.
OR
I'm just worried.

My father's a doctor.
OR
My father's sick.

That's OK.
OR
Thanks.

3. Circle the Answer

1. A: ....
      a) I could put an ad in the newspaper.   b) Where did you get your sweater?
      c) How do I get to the newspaper office?
    B: Take the bus on Broadway and get off at 42nd Street.

2. A: ....
      a) Why don't you get a roommate?   b) Why don't you go home and go to bed?
      c) Why did you go home?
    B: I can't. I have to meet Tomiko.

3. A: ....
      a) What's wrong?   b) What did you do?   c) What are you doing?
    B: I'm in a bad mood.

4. A: ....
      a) How do I get to Macy's?   b) Do you know where I can get a sweater?
      c) Do you know where Macy's is?
    B: Uh-huh. It's on the corner of Broadway and 34th.

5. A: ....
      a) I don't like my apartment.   b) I don't like the subway.   c) I don't like New York.
    B: Why don't you take the bus?

LANGUAGE SUMMARY

Now You Can Do This:

talk about how you feel:	What's the matter? Oh, I'm just depressed. I still haven't found a job. Nothing.
make a suggestion:	Why don't you get a roommate?
accept a suggestion:	That's not a bad idea.
reject a suggestion:	No, I don't want to.
ask for and give locations:	Do you know where the *New York News* is? It's on the corner of Broadway and 38th Street.
ask for and give directions:	How do I get to the *New York News?* Take the subway to 42nd Street and you can walk from there.

Grammar

Imperative

Take the subway.
Get off at 42nd Street.

Word Order of Embedded Questions

Where **is** the *New York News?*
Do you know where the *New York News* **is?**

Still

I **still** haven't found a job.

Useful Words and Expressions

move
get off
•
fight
mood
roommate
•
depressed

•
still
soon
•
Hmmm.
That's not a bad idea.
What's wrong?
Not very well.

Saturday in New York.

PRACTICE 1 Read the ad from the newspaper and answer the questions.

1. A realtor

   a) helps people find a place to live.
   b) goes sightseeing with people.
   c) helps people find roommates.

2. A studio is probably

   a) not the same as a one-bedroom apartment.
   b) the same as a one-bedroom apartment.
   c) the same as a two-bedroom apartment.

3. Village Realtors has

   a) apartments only in Greenwich Village.
   b) houses and apartments in Manhattan.
   c) furnished apartments in Manhattan.

Jim is looking for an apartment when he meets Maria in Washington Square.
Maria has just finished running.

JIM: Hi, Maria. How have you been?

MARIA: Fine, Mr. Chapman. And you?

JIM: Fine. Listen, call me Jim, OK?

MARIA: OK. What are you doing around here on Saturday?

JIM: I'm looking for an apartment in the neighborhood and there were a couple of ads in the paper this morning.

MARIA: Oh, really? What kind of apartment are you looking for?

JIM: I need two bedrooms, but everything's so expensive! I don't think I'm going to find anything.

MARIA: How long have you been looking?

JIM: Only a couple of weeks. Do you run here every day?

MARIA: Yes, but I usually run at night when it's not so crowded.

JIM: I was just reading an article in the paper about all the midnight joggers. Did you see it?

MARIA: No.

JIM: Oh, it's right here somewhere. Yeah, here it is.

Answer *That's right* **or** *That's wrong.*

1. Jim is looking for an apartment near Washington Square.

2. Jim has been looking for an apartment for two weeks.

3. *Jogging* means "running."

PRACTICE 2 Greet someone.

JIM: Hi, Maria. How have you been?

MARIA: Fine. And you?

JIM: Fine.

A: Hi, ... How have you been?

B: .... And you?

A: ....

PRACTICE 3   Talk about something you're looking for.

JIM: I'm looking for an apartment in the neighborhood.
MARIA: What kind of apartment are you looking for?
JIM: I need two bedrooms.

A: I'm looking for ....
B: What kind of .... are you looking for?
A: ....

PRACTICE 4   Complete the article. Use some of these words.

morning   said
people   took
night
they   it's

are   on
has   at
was
don't   the
can   a

NEW YORK NEWS   **Thursday, October 23, 1979**

In the last few years Washington Square _____ become the favorite place to run for people living in Greenwich Village. _____ almost impossible to go there and not see _____ runner—even _____ two or three o'clock in the _____! "There _____ too many _____ in the daytime," said one midnight jogger. "Late at _____ I'm alone, except, of course, for the other joggers." When asked if they thought it _____ dangerous to run so late at night, most of the joggers _____ no. "Everyone knows joggers _____ carry any money."

Bad weather doesn't stop the joggers either. _____ even run in the rain and the snow.

PRACTICE 5   Complete the conversation and practice it with a partner.

JIM: Why don't we go get something to eat?

MARIA: ....
1. That's wrong.
2. That sounds like a good idea.
3. That's all right.

JIM: ....
1. Where is it?
2. Where are you going?
3. Where would you like to go?

MARIA: ....
1. What about Amy's restaurant?
2. What about you?
3. Thank you.

JIM: ....
1. Fine, do you mind if we stop at a bookstore on the way?
2. Fine, do you mind if we go to a restaurant?
3. Fine, do you mind if I talk to you?

MARIA: ....
1. Not you. We can go to the Marlboro Bookstore.
2. Not at all. We can go to the Marlboro Bookstore.
3. Not yet. We can go to the Marlboro Bookstore.

Jim and Maria are at Amy's Restaurant.

JIM: What do you usually do on weekends besides run?

MARIA: Oh, I go to the movies or the theater. Sometimes I go to Boston. I have some friends there.

JIM: How do you get there?

MARIA: I take the train.

JIM: I've never been there. How long does it take?

MARIA: About three hours. There's a restaurant on the train, and I can read. I really enjoy it.

JIM: I'd like to do that sometime. Maybe next weekend. I haven't taken a train in years and it sounds like fun. The kids would like it too.

MARIA: Yeah. They'd love it.

Answer *That's right* **or** *That's wrong.*

1. Maria goes to the movies every weekend.

2. Jim usually travels by train.

3. Jim has one child.

PRACTICE 6 Talk about what you usually do on weekends.

JIM: What do you usually do on weekends?
MARIA: I go to the movies or the theater.

A: What do you usually do ....?
B: I/We ....

PRACTICE 7 Talk about places you visit and how you get there.

MARIA: Sometimes I go to Boston.
JIM: How do you get there?
MARIA: I take the train.
JIM: How long does it take?
MARIA: About three hours.

A: Sometimes I go ....
B: How do you get there?
A: ....
B: How long does it take?
A: About ....

PRACTICE 8 Complete the conversation and practice it with a partner.

WAITRESS: Can I get you anything?

MARIA: ....
1. Do you have to go?
2. Do you have chocolate cake?
3. Do you have to study?

WAITRESS: ....
1. Sure.
2. Vanilla ice cream.
3. Is it expensive?

MARIA: ....
1. I'd like a piece of cake and a cup of coffee.
2. With cream.
3. No sugar, please.

WAITRESS: ....
1. See you later.
2. Let's go.
3. All right.

MARIA: ....
1. Oh, and where's that?
2. Oh, and where's the coffee?
3. Oh, and where's the ladies' room?

WAITRESS: ....
1. Next to the ladies' room?
2. Next to the telephone.
3. Next week.

MARIA: ....
1. Goodbye.
2. Thank you.
3. That's OK.

PRACTICE 9

After Jim leaves Maria, he goes home and writes a letter. Read the letter and answer the questions.

1. In line (2) *we* refers to

   a) Jim and his mother.
   b) Jim and his children.
   c) the children and their friends.

2. In line (4) *they* refers to

   a) the children.
   b) the children's friends.
   c) New York and Los Angeles.

3. In lines (7) and (8) *It's just difficult being single again* means

   a) Jim is married now.
   b) Jim isn't married now.
   c) Jim's wife is in Los Angeles.

4. In line (12) *it* refers to

   a) the weekend.
   b) the train.
   c) the trip to Boston.

5. In lines (16) and (17) *I want to go to the store before the kids come home from swimming lessons* means

   a) the kids are coming home and then Jim is going to the store.
   b) Jim is going to the store and then the kids are coming home.
   c) Jim and the kids are going to the store when the kids come home.

PRACTICE 10

Jim forgot to tell his mother something, so he added a *P.S.* to his letter. Find the sentences that continue the idea of the paragraph. Write them. The sentences are in the right order.

Did you find the papers I left?
Washington Square is 88 years old this year.
I've been looking for two weeks now, and I can't find an apartment I can afford.
They're so expensive in Greenwich Village.
Movies are so expensive these days.
I only pay $350.00 a month for a two-bedroom apartment now and a two-bedroom apartment in the Village is $550.00!
She paid $350.00 last year.
I'm going to keep looking, but it's kind of depressing.
I'm depressed because I lost my job.
My friend, Tom, is looking for a new car too.

JC

(1) Dear Mom,
How are things in Los Angeles? We're all fine here. The kids have made friends now and they like school. I think they've (5) even forgotten they didn't want to move to New York. I'm still a little lonely, but I guess that's normal. It's just difficult being single again.
I like my job and the people I work (10) with, and I have a lot of free time. Next weekend we're going to take a trip to Boston. It'll be the kids' first train ride and I'm sure they'll love it. I haven't been on a train in a long time, so I'm (15) looking forward to it too!
Well, I have to go now. I want to go to the store before the kids come home from swimming lessons. I'll mail this on the way. Take care of yourself (20) and don't forget we're waiting for your visit.
Love,
Jim
P.S. I almost forgot, I'm still (25) trying to find an apartment near Washington Square, but I think it's going to be impossible. _____

After Maria leaves Jim Chapman, she calls Tomiko.

TOMIKO:	Hello?
MARIA:	Hi, Tomiko. This is Maria.
TOMIKO:	Oh, hi, Maria. How are you?
MARIA:	Fine. What are you doing?
TOMIKO:	Just reading. What about you?
MARIA:	I just got home. I had lunch with Jim . . . uh, Mr. Chapman.
TOMIKO:	Oh, really?
MARIA:	Yeah. I'll tell you about it later. . . . Say, what're you going to do tonight?
TOMIKO:	Nothing special. Why?
MARIA:	Some friends are coming over later and we're going to watch that TV special, *America Sings*. Would you and Tony like to come?

TOMIKO:	Sure. What time?
MARIA:	Oh, about 7:30.
TOMIKO:	OK. Lynn just made an apple pie. I'll bring some.
MARIA:	Great. See you later.
TOMIKO:	Bye-bye.

Answer *That's right* **or** *That's wrong.*

1. Tomiko is writing a letter.

2. Some friends are going to Maria's house.

3. Tomiko made an apple pie.

PRACTICE 11 Begin a telephone conversation and ask someone what he's/she's doing.

TOMIKO:	Hello?
MARIA:	Hi, Tomiko. This is Maria.
TOMIKO:	Oh, hi, Maria. How are you?
MARIA:	Fine. What are you doing?
TOMIKO:	Just reading.

A:	Hello?
B:	Hi, ... This is ....
A:	Oh, hi, ... How are you?
B:	.... What are you doing?
A:	I ....

111

PRACTICE 12

Ask someone what he's/she's going to do tonight/tomorrow/next week.
Say what you're going to do.

MARIA: What're you going to do tonight?
TOMIKO: Nothing special.

A: What're you going to do ....?
B: ....

PRACTICE 13

Invite someone to do something.
Accept an invitation and ask what time.

MARIA: We're going to watch that TV special. Would you like to come?
TOMIKO: Sure. What time?
MARIA: About 7:30.

A: I'm/We're going to .... Would you like to come/go?
B: Sure. What time?
A: ....

PRACTICE 14

Tomiko calls Tony to ask him to go to Maria's.
Complete their conversation.

TOMIKO: Would you like to go to Maria's to watch
a TV special?

TONY: ....
1. How?
2. How much?
3. What time?

TOMIKO: ....
1. 30 minutes.
2. 7:30.
3. For two hours.

TONY: ....
1. All right. Can I bring anything?
2. That's too bad. Can I bring anything?
3. I'm sorry. Can I bring anything?

TOMIKO: ....
1. I'm taking a bookcase. Why don't you bring a desk?
2. I'm sick. Why don't you bring some aspirin?
3. I'm taking some apple pie. Why don't you bring some ice cream?

TONY: ....
1. That sounds like a good idea. When?
2. That sounds like a good idea. What kind?
3. That sounds like a good idea. Where?

TOMIKO: ....
1. Vanilla.
2. Blond.
3. Interesting.

TONY: ....
1. Fine, thank you.
2. OK. See you later.
3. That's awful. Goodbye.

PRACTICE 15   Read the *TV guide* and answer *True* or *False*.

1. All the programs are at the same time.   T   F

2. Vicky Fitzgerald, Alan King and Jack Cook are musicians or singers.   T   F

3. "Today in Review" is a new movie.   T   F

4. The eight-year-old boy doesn't have a mother.   T   F

5. Romeo and Juliet lived in the 13th century.   T   F

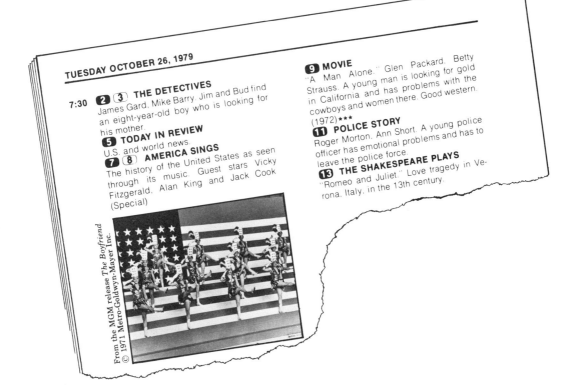

TUESDAY OCTOBER 26, 1979

7:30   **2 3 THE DETECTIVES**
James Gard, Mike Barry. Jim and Bud find an eight-year-old boy who is looking for his mother.
5 TODAY IN REVIEW
U.S. and world news.
7 8 AMERICA SINGS
The history of the United States as seen through its music. Guest stars Vicky Fitzgerald, Alan King and Jack Cook (Special)

9 MOVIE
"A Man Alone." Glen Packard. Betty Strauss. A young man is looking for gold in California and has problems with the cowboys and women there. Good western. (1972)★★★
11 POLICE STORY
Roger Morton. Ann Short. A young police officer has emotional problems and has to leave the police force.
13 THE SHAKESPEARE PLAYS
"Romeo and Juliet." Love tragedy in Verona. Italy. in the 13th century.

From the MGM release *The Boyfriend*.
© 1971 Metro-Goldwyn-Mayer Inc.

PRACTICE 16   Complete Tomiko's note to her cousin and his wife Lynn. Use some of these words.

TV
the children
the radio

going
be
were
take

late
apple
happy
new

a
an

Lynn and Toshi,

    I'm _____ to Maria's to watch _____. There's a special on tonight. I'll probably _____ home about 12:00, but don't worry if I'm _____. I'll _____ a taxi. I took some of the _____ pie. I hope you don't mind. I hope you enjoyed the movie. See you later.

Tomiko

PRACTICE 17 Do the crossword puzzle.

ACROSS

2. Saturday and Sunday.
5. Another word for work.
6. A number.
8. A telephone ....
9. Someone you live with. Not a relative.
11. Do you .... go to the ballet?
12. The present of *went*.
13. Do you want apple, lemon .... chocolate pie?
14. Another time.
15. Where are you ....?
16. No, ... I don't smoke.
19. Not happy.

DOWN

1. If you don't have any money, you can .... some from a friend.
2. A question word.
3. A room.
4. An auxiliary.
6. The day after today.
7. A color.
9. The opposite of wrong.
10. What's the ....? Are you sick?
14. An article.
15. I've been here .... two months.
17. I have a runny ....
18. A possessive adjective.
20. 4 DOWN.

Now You Can Do This

UNIT 1

introduce people:
Tony, I'd like you to meet Grace Richards.
It's nice to meet you, Mrs. Richards.

ask and say how long:
How long have you been here?
For about three months.

identify other people:
Who's that? Do you know him?
Uh-huh. That's Tony Costa.

ask and say what other people do:
What does he do?
He studies English at New York University.

ask and tell someone the time:
Do you know what time it is? It's 9:15.

say you have to leave and say why:
I've got to go. I've got to meet Tomiko at 9:30.

say goodbye to people you've just met:
It was nice to meet you, Mrs. Richards.
Nice to meet you too, Tony.

UNIT 2

talk about sickness:
I don't feel very well.
What's the matter?
I have a cold.
I hope you feel better.
Thanks.

say you don't feel like doing something:
I don't feel like going to class today.

make a suggestion:
Why don't you go home and go to bed?
Maybe you should see a doctor.

accept a suggestion:
That's a good idea.

reject a suggestion:
No, I'll be OK.

make a request:
Could you give this note to Mr. Chapman?

agree to a request:
Sure. I'd be glad to.

UNIT 3

ask for and give information
about the past:
Where were you last Friday?
I was sick so I didn't come to class.

Did you have a nice weekend?
Yes, I went to the Bears' game.

ask for and give
an opinion:
How was class on Friday?
It was kind of boring.

Was the movie good?
It was great./We really enjoyed it.

UNIT 4

talk about the past:
What did you do this weekend? I went sightseeing.

make a suggestion:
Why don't we go to the World Trade Center next weekend?
Let's go to Chinatown.

accept a suggestion:
That's a good idea.

say you can't accept a suggestion:
I can't next weekend/tonight/tomorrow.

UNIT 5

ask for and give an opinion:
How do you like New York? I really like it. It's exciting.

What do you think of Rose?
I like her. I think she's a lot of fun./
I don't like her. I think she's selfish and rude.

ask for and give descriptions:
What does he look like?
He's tall and fat, wears glasses and has a mustache.

give and accept compliments:
That's a beautiful dress. Thank you.

UNIT 6

say you need something:
I need a desk.

ask where you can get something:
Do you know where I can get a bookcase?

say where someone can get something:
They have desks on sale at Macy's.

make a suggestion:
Why don't you call Macy's?

talk about prices:
How much are they/is it? About $110.00.

talk about something you've lost or found:
I lost/found a sweater the other day. Where did you lose/find it?

UNIT 7

invite someone to do something:
I'm having a party tomorrow night. Would you like to come?

accept an invitation:
Sure.

ask and say what time:
What time? Any time after eight.

ask for and give permission:
Do you mind if I bring a friend? No, not at all.

make a request:	Could I borrow your stereo?	
accept a request:	Sure.	
refuse a request:	I'm sorry, I don't have one./I'm sorry, I need it.	
offer to do something:	Do you want me to bring some records?	
accept an offer:	That'd be nice.	
refuse an offer:	No, I don't think so.	

UNIT 8

start a conversation:	How have you been? Just fine. And you? OK, I guess.
offer something to someone:	Would you like a cigarette?
accept an offer:	Yes, thank you./Yes, please.
refuse an offer:	No, thank you. I don't smoke.
offer to get something for someone:	Can I get you anything?
make a request:	Do you have any orange juice?
accept/refuse a request:	Sure./I'm sorry. I don't have any orange juice.
apologize:	I'm sorry I'm late./Oh, I'm sorry!
accept an apology:	That's all right./Don't worry about it./It doesn't matter.

UNIT 9

talk about how to get places:	How do you get to work? I take the bus./I go by train./I walk.
ask and say how long it takes to go somewhere:	How long does it take you to get to the airport? About half an hour./Not very long.
talk about what people usually do:	What do you usually do on weekends? I always play tennis on Saturday morning, but my afternoons are free. Do you ever go to the ballet? No, not very often.

UNIT 10

start a telephone conversation:	Hello? Hello. Is Tony there? This is Tony. Hi, Tony. This is Tomiko.
offer to take a telephone message:	I'm sorry, he's busy right now. Can I take a message?
leave a telephone message:	Please tell him Tony called.
talk about the present:	What are you doing? Waiting for Paula. What are you doing? Nothing much.
talk about the future:	What are you going to do later? I'm going to see *Superman*.
invite someone to do something:	Would you like to meet us for dinner?
refuse an invitation:	I can't. I'm going to see *Superman* with Ali./ Thank you, but I can't.

UNIT 11

invite someone to do something:	I'm going to get something to eat. Do you want to come?
accept an invitation:	Sure./That sounds like a good idea.
refuse an invitation:	No, I'm not hungry./No, thank you. I just ate.
talk about problems:	You look worried. Is anything wrong? I lost my job.
sympathize:	That's too bad./I'm sorry to hear that.
ask and say how long:	How long have you been looking for a job? For about a week.

UNIT 12

talk about how you feel:	What's the matter? Oh, I'm just depressed. I still haven't found a job. Nothing.
make a suggestion:	Why don't you get a roommate?
accept a suggestion:	That's not a bad idea.
reject a suggestion:	No, I don't want to.
ask for and give locations:	Do you know where the *New York News* is? It's on the corner of Broadway and 38th Street.
ask for and give directions:	How do I get to the *New York News?* Take the subway to 42nd Street and you can walk from there.

Grammar Index

Irregular Verbs

Base Form*	Past Tense	Past Participle	Base Form*	Past Tense	Past Participle
be	was / were	been	let	let	let
beat	beat	beaten	lie	lay	lain
become	became	become	light	lit	lit
begin	began	begun	lose	lost	lost
bend	bent	bent	make	made	made
bet	bet	bet	mean	meant	meant
bite	bit	bitten	meet	met	met
blow	blew	blown	put	put	put
break	broke	broken	quit	quit	quit
bring	brought	brought	read	read	read
build	built	built	ride	rode	ridden
buy	bought	bought	ring	rang	rung
catch	caught	caught	rise	rose	risen
choose	chose	chosen	run	ran	run
come	came	come	say	said	said
cost	cost	cost	see	saw	seen
cut	cut	cut	sell	sold	sold
dig	dug	dug	send	sent	sent
do	did	done	set	set	set
draw	drew	drawn	shake	shook	shaken
drink	drank	drunk	shine	shone	shone
drive	drove	driven	shoot	shot	shot
eat	ate	eaten	shut	shut	shut
fall	fell	fallen	sing	sang	sung
feed	fed	fed	sink	sank	sunk
feel	felt	felt	sit	sat	sat
fight	fought	fought	sleep	slept	slept
find	found	found	slide	slid	slid
fit	fit	fit	speak	spoke	spoken
fly	flew	flown	spend	spent	spent
forget	forgot	forgotten	stand	stood	stood
freeze	froze	frozen	steal	stole	stolen
get	got	gotten	stick	stuck	stuck
give	gave	given	strike	struck	struck
go	went	gone	swear	swore	sworn
hang	hung	hung	sweep	swept	swept
have	had	had	swim	swam	swum
hear	heard	heard	take	took	taken
hide	hid	hidden	teach	taught	taught
hit	hit	hit	tear	tore	torn
hold	held	held	tell	told	told
hurt	hurt	hurt	think	thought	thought
keep	kept	kept	throw	threw	thrown
know	knew	known	understand	understood	understood
lay	laid	laid	wake	woke	woke / woken
lead	led	led	wear	wore	worn
leave	left	left	win	won	won
lend	lent	lent	write	wrote	written

* infinitive = to + base form (to be, to give, etc.)

Word List

The number beside each word tells you where the word first appears in the book. This Word List does not include words that first appeared in Student's Book 1.

A

accidentally 68
according 12
act (v) 68
active 56
ad 39
adjective 14
afford 34
airport 73
ambulance 84
ancient 27
anniversary 69
another 43
anymore 97
anything 17
anyway 42
apologize 68
apply 92
architecture 93
area 49
arm 4
arrive 68
artist 27
as 49
aspirin 10
assailant 77
assignment 13
assistance 84
attractive 4
audience 52
auxiliary 114
awful 13

B

backache 10
bad 4
ball 20
ballet 73
banking 34
bar 27
basket 21
basketball 21
bathroom 60
beat 20
beautiful 27
become 20
bed 9
been 1
began 20
beige 41
below 5
besides 108
best 20

bet (v) 75
bicycle 43
big 36
bike 43
birthday 54
black 33
blond 33
blouse 33
blue 39
board 39
bookcase 39
borrow 39
boss 73
bother 4
box 5
boy 53
break (v) 67
bridge 31
bring 57
brown 33
bucket 59
build 27
bulletin 39
burn (v) 10
button 39
bus 28
buy (v) 49

C

cabinet 67
call (v) 13
capitalize 77
car 44
carry 76
cat 43
cause (v) 56
center 21
century 113
championship 20
charges 84
cheaper 84
checked 41
church 49
cigarette 65
circle 4
citizen 93
classmate 56
clear 27
close (adj.) 4
close (v) 83
club 31
coach 21
code 84
coin 84

cold 4
collar 41
collect 84
color 43
combined 34
comfortable 23
community 27
completely 92
condition 40
contact 43
cost 34
counter 67
country 4
couple 1
court 21
cowboy 113
cracker 66
crazy 76
cream 109
crime 35
criticize 4
crowded 32
crutch 76
culture 27
curly 32
custom 49
cut (v) 10

D

dangerous 34
dark 36
daytime 107
deck 27
degree 93
deposit 84
depressed 92
depressing 100
description 40
desk 39
dial 84
diarrhea 13
did 17
didn't 17
differently 68
difficult 34
diplomatic 4
dirty 31
disaster 76
distance 84
doesn't 3
doorbell 65
drive (v) 74
during 75

E

each 4
earache 10
early 48
editor 76
educational 93
electrician 55
embarrassed 4
emergency 84
emotional 113
employer 92
employment 92
end (v) 21
enjoy 17
enough 34
everybody 4
everyone 4
everywhere 76
exchange (v) 43
excitement 52
expenses 43
explain 4

F

famous 12
far 73
fascinating 27
fat 31
feast 49
feel 4
feel like 9
feet (foot) 27
fever 12
fight 98
final 20
fire 84
fix 36
force 113
forget 52
fortunately 35
forward 20
friendly 37
friendship 4
fun 30
furnished 105
furniture 40

G

gee 9
general 4
get up 70
gift 27
glasses 31